Walk in Beauty

KELLI BROOKER

© **Kelli Brooker, 2023**

Disclaimer

The material in this publication is of the nature of general comment only and does not represent professional advice. It is not intended to provide specific guidance for any particular circumstances, and it should not be relied upon for any decision to take action or not to take action on any matter that it covers. To the maximum extent permitted by law, the author and publisher disclaim all responsibility and liability to any person, arising directly or indirectly from any person taking or not taking action based on the information in this book.

ISBN: pbk: 978-0-6458816-0-8

First published August 2023 by Kelli Brooker, www.MoonstoneGypsyAU.com

All rights reserved. Except as permitted under the *Australian Copyright Act 1968* (for example, fair dealing for the purposes of study, research, criticism or review), no part of this book may be reproduced, stored in a retrieval system, communicated or transmitted in any form or by any means without prior written permission. All inquiries should be made to the publisher.

Editing and design by Claire McGregor, Kookaburra Hill Publishing Services, www.clairemcgregor.com.au

Illustrations by Pixabay: Sandro Ruiti, b0red, Gordon Johnson, Michael Hourigan, InspiredImages, OpenClipart-Vectors.

Dedication and acknowledgements

Hey dreamers,

I am here for the mystics, free spirits, healers, artists, witches and bohemians of our world.

I give so much love and thanks to my family for their support, patience and encouragement during this new journey I have embarked upon.

I extend love and gratitude to my spirit guides, Gray Wolf with his feather prompts for me, my ancestors, and my animal guides, Spirit Bear and Little Wolf.

I also need to mention Karine, a trusted psychic medium who for years has provided me with valuable insights and blessings and has reminded me that I hold the key to my power, and the world is my oyster!

Walk in Beauty

As I walk, as I walk
The universe is walking with me
In beauty it walks before me
In beauty it walks behind me
In beauty it walks below me
In beauty it walks above me.
Beauty is on every side
As I walk, I walk with beauty.

Traditional Navajo prayer

Contents

Moonchild beginnings   **1**

Chapter 1
Working with your crystals   *9*

Chapter 2
Crystal shapes   *22*

Chapter 3
Cleanse, charge and program   *37*

Chapter 4
Chakras, auras and crystals   *46*

Chapter 5
Healing everyday ailments with crystals   *65*

Chapter 6
Smudging with sacred herbs   *79*

Chapter 7
Everyday self-care   *92*

Chapter 8
Working with the moon phases — *114*

Chapter 9
Reiki energy healing — *133*

Chapter 10
Negative energy and psychic vampires — *147*

Chapter 11
Support from the higher realms and Great Spirit — *164*

Chapter 12
Making magick with candles — *182*

Chapter 13
Practising divination — *191*

A'ho — **201**
About the author — **203**

Moonchild beginnings

Let's travel back to the birth and creation of MoonstoneGypsyAU...

It all began on the new moon of October 2016 when nothing more than an intuitive thought flowed through me during a meditation session. I have no idea who the voice belonged to or whether it was a guide, an ancestor or even a beloved family member who had crossed over. I honestly cannot say whose voice it was I heard to this day, but it prompted me into my next life phase and learning.

I was in my early 40s when I started delving into the world of spirituality and crystals. I purchased my tumble stones and books from a local new-age crystal store. One morning the store owner offered me a free crystal healing session with a lady who needed to fill her practical hours to qualify for her Diploma in Healing. I was more than willing to give it a go, so I accepted with gratitude. I didn't know what to expect but, it turns out, it was my lucky day.

# Walk in Beauty

A few minutes later, out walked a bohemian goddess rocking rainbow-coloured dreads, an ample, curvaceous body, bare feet, and amazing energy that had me feeling euphoric before she even touched me! I was still a tad nervous though. She guided me into her little room, had me lie down comfortably and then proceeded to put on music.

To my delight, she chose Native American drumming, which resonated with me immediately as, I am proud to say, I have Cherokee blood coursing through my veins, and this part of my family still reside in North Carolina, USA, to this day.

Over the next 30 minutes, I found myself nearly falling asleep but also slipping deeper into a meditative state listening to the heartbeat of the music and feeling it pulsate through my heart and body. Needless to say, half an hour of crystal energy and healing rocked my world (pun intended)!

After the healing, we shared the biggest hug imaginable. Usually, I'm not a touchy-feely person, especially to strangers, but she had changed that ... it was like she was magick! I walked out feeling uplifted and light as a feather, and excitedly told my husband, Wayne, I was going to become a crystal healer, just like her.

I used to buy crystals online, but they weren't exactly cheap, so I didn't have a large collection or know too much about them. However, one night, my daughter Ashley and I were scrolling through social media when an astrophyllite wand popped up, and I was compelled to buy it on the spot. I was adamant I had to have that wand right now, despite not knowing what the crystal was or what it did.

Fast forward several days later, after receiving my wand and incorporating it into my evening meditation sessions, something magickal happened ... I clearly heard a voice tell me I needed to start a crystal business to share with the world, and to become a healer. I was so excited as I had never heard anything so precise in my life, and I knew I had to follow through.

The more I read about astrophyllite, the more I knew it was meant to find and inspire me on my journey. Astrophyllite is a stone of astrology and star wisdom, which helps connect us with higher realms. When used during meditation, it can provide insight and ideas for the future. It also helps us with life transitions, when challenging or positive changes arise in our path, or when we reach a crossroads and become stuck. Astrophyllite propels us forward on our life path and helps us to see the bigger picture unfolding.

 Walk in Beauty

Perhaps by coincidence, astrophyllite guides us in a direction that allows us to cross paths and meet certain people along the way, who teach us valuable lessons about trust, friendship, authenticity and betrayal. I have certainly evolved over the past several years and encountered many ups and downs along the way.

Next came the daunting task of starting an e-commerce business, which I had no idea about besides my love for crystals and all things spiritual. Enter my darling husband, Wayne, who is smart with business, importing, managing taxes and finances. It's a perfect match already, isn't it? I soon learnt the ropes of running a business and everything that happens behind the scenes, which most people think looks easy ... Nothing is further from the truth.

I aspired to be authentic, truthful and ethical in my business, so I had to educate myself in all aspects of crystals and how they worked. I didn't want to use second-hand information from multiple sources as I found it conflicting and confusing.

My goal was to help people without relying on the internet or others for answers, and I was passionate about attaining an internationally recognised qualification in crystal healing. From the beginning, I wasn't interested in making a quick dollar as I knew my purpose was to help guide and heal others on their spiritual journey.

I studied extensively for 12 months to attain my Crystal Healing Diploma, and for those who don't believe it's a true qualification or skill, so be it. The comprehensive crystal history and metaphysical information I learnt turned me into a walking encyclopaedia of crystal knowledge, chakras, healings and all things spiritual.

Seven years later, I'm still learning new information and have an open mind to everything that crosses my path because knowledge is power, and I believe this is why our business has succeeded for this long. I love healing others with Reiki and offering recommendations and advice on how to intuitively choose and use crystals to their fullest potential. I am confident and ethical in everything I do, and I feel our lovely customers recognise and appreciate this.

It took years to reach where we are today and, in the beginning, I worked countless hours on the laptop with no sales or income to reflect all the work I was investing into the business. I often wondered if I had made a big mistake. Regardless, I started a business page on Facebook to advertise our crystals, and my only supporters were close family and friends. However, I kept persevering as I loved crystals, and I knew I had clearly heard my spirit guides that night, and I never doubt higher spiritual energy, dreams or intuitive insights.

 Walk in Beauty

As I mentioned, I had no idea about the financial side of the business, or how to create a website for that matter. Along came our youngest daughter, Ashley, who is an absolute legend with technology. She designed a website and uploaded all the crystals and spiritual creations I had photographed and written descriptions for. The entire process took a long time to perfect, and to this day Ashley still manages the technological side of the business for us.

Then slowly it happened ... I received my first sale, even if it was from a dear friend who I still have to this day (thank you, Anna). I was so excited to hear the initial *cha-ching* on my phone, I danced a happy dance and it seemed to work! Sales started rolling in, and crystals were being sent to their new homes, so I felt I must be doing something right.

Fast forward several years and MoonstoneGypsyAU has become such a success. I could no longer handle the workload and long hours by myself, so our family took a leap of faith and sold our house of 20 years to buy a smaller house with larger land in the Sunshine Coast Hinterland. I had always dreamed of living in the Hinterland after frequent visits over the years, and we were blessed to have found a little house upon a hill that has the most wonderful view of the mountains. For us, it feels like we are living the dream.

My family said goodbye to their previous jobs, and we packed up the truck and have not looked back since. Yes, of course, we have arguments about work; the reality is we are women, and Wayne is the only male in the mix. He is the peacekeeper in our household and family business because, let's face it, to disagree and occasionally argue is normal human behaviour.

We aren't perfect by any means, but passion, teamwork and dedication are what we have, and it works. Our Whippet girls encourage us to stop and smell the flowers along the way, take breaks, drink coffee (which I always share with them), play ball and venture outside on the grass barefoot when the pressure and busyness becomes too much.

I count my blessings every day, and we are incredibly grateful to have achieved everything we have so far. So, from the bottom of my heart, I extend my thanks and gratitude to each and every person who has supported our business journey.

A few of you mentioned to me that I should write a book … well, here it is! So, sit back and allow me to share insights, knowledge and stories with you all.

 Walk in Beauty

We Do Not Want Riches

... I am poor and naked, but I am the Chief of the nation.

We do not want riches but we

do want to train our children right.

Riches would do us no good.

We could not take them with us to the other world.

We do not want riches.

We want love and peace.

**Chief Red Cloud (Makhpiya-Luta),
late 19th century. Lakota Sioux.**

Chapter 1

Working with your crystals

Crystals have long been admired as pretty rocks, gems and minerals, but they are also so much more. I'm a firm believer of treating them with respect so they may share their infinite energy vibration with us during healings and daily life. For this to happen, we need to establish a connection with our crystals, and, for me, this entails always caring for them before and after every healing I use them for.

You don't have to be a crystal healer to help yourself at home; everyone can heal themselves with their special magickal crystals. My life purpose is to help you realise your inner potential and natural ability to work with these beautiful gifts from Mother Earth.

Every day I'm here to advise, guide and help you choose the exact crystal fit for your current health, energy, ailment or wish. And, let's be honest, it can be daunting with the

 Walk in Beauty

extensive amount of information out there on the internet. There is an abundance of false information, but also a lot that is true. So, how do you know what advice to follow? I always suggest going with a book. The author obviously has a passion and love for their work, so much so they dedicated their time to writing down their tips, experiences and knowledge to share with us all.

Thankfully, crystals have become so much more accepted these days, and the majority of people don't automatically label you a hippie, witch or freak for delving into spirituality, crystals and the metaphysical world. Not that I mind the name-calling as I feel it stems from a place of fear of the unknown and an unwillingness people have to open their minds and dig deeper into truly understanding the ancient healing powers and practices of crystals.

Crystals have expanded beyond spiritual tools and are often used as home décor and accessories that spark joy in our lives. As a result of crystals gaining popularity across the world, they are now readily available in a variety of places, such as market stalls, discount shops, retail stores and online businesses. It's important to always check whether the crystals are ethically sourced because being mindful makes a difference.

Chapter 1

We want to appreciate crystals and work with their energy, but we also need to protect our Mother Earth from over-mining and unethical practices. Unfortunately, this is sadly the case, with quite a few crystals becoming exhausted and extinct from extensive mining and lack of consideration for nature and her crystal formations.

As an ethical family business, we choose to work with trusted suppliers we have built a strong relationship with over the past several years. With weekly communication and video streams of crystals being sourced and carved by our suppliers, we take pride in the process of our crystals from start to finish.

We are often questioned about our pricing structure in comparison to other businesses as our prices are often considerably lower. This has nothing to do with the quality; rather, it has to do with our ethical and spiritual morals about keeping crystals affordable for everyone embarking on their spiritual journey. I'm not driven by money; sure, it's nice to have financial security, but what makes my heart sing is the joy of someone who can finally afford a crystal they will love and cherish. The messages and photos I receive weekly from friends and customers are my rewards.

 Walk in Beauty

The four main elements of crystals

By being mindful, patient and respectful to the crystal you are working with, you will find that, just as they do for me, their energy will have a positive and beneficial effect on you. When working with crystals, there are 4 main elements of our wellbeing and life that the energies connect with:

1. *Expanding our spiritual awareness.* For those who love meditation, intuition, divination and have a keen interest in awakening their third eye chakra, there is nothing more mystical than delving into the higher spiritual realms, to see how it all works and what exists in these alternate planes. In the higher realms, there is no concept of time, for it's irrelevant in the spirit world. Crystals are powerful tools in our spiritual journey that help us become more open to the messages, signs and predictions from our spirit guides and spirit animals.

2. *Developing balance and stability.* Crystals are wonderful for releasing stagnant energy and blocks from our physical and etheric bodies. Use grounding crystals to balance the yin–yang energies flowing through your body and to strengthen your energy system (chakras). Balance is everything when it comes to our bodies, and integrating crystals into self-care practices can have a beneficial impact on our daily living and wellbeing.

3. *Clearing our energy.* We use crystals to clear the way! It's normal for negative and blocked energy to reside within us as we experience stress, psychic vampires, mood swings and triggers daily. Crystals help to clear and recharge our bodies by merging with our energy to help raise our spiritual vibration. The higher our vibration, the more aligned our health and emotions will be.

4. *Supporting health ailments.* Crystals will never cure serious illnesses and ailments, but they will help ease our thoughts and reactions to pains and aches. I use crystals for my health issues, and they vastly improve my feelings and outlook on life. I have had many customers report the same.

For health issues like headaches, overthinking, bad dreams, restlessness, inability to sleep, needless worry, etc., we can experience a significant turnaround if the source of our symptoms stems from a stagnant mindset and unbalanced energy. I've outlined all the crystals relevant to these points later.

 Walk in Beauty

Choosing crystals

This is simpler than you may realise – trust your intuition! Don't allow the size, shape or colour comparison to influence your decision when choosing crystals though because perfect and large crystals are overrated. In all honesty, I always choose a "faulty" crystal. Out of a batch of 25 spheres, for example, I'm more likely to be intuitively drawn to the one with a break, hole, surface crack or a pattern that is not as pretty compared to the others.

Generally, I choose crystals within an instant of seeing them because I go with my gut every time instead of overthinking and scrutinising each one. I realise that buying online can make it hard for those who want to pick up every individual crystal, but, truth be told, you honestly don't have to touch a crystal to connect with it. It's often love at first sight!

Coincidently (I don't believe in coincidences by the way; I feel many events in our lives are destined to unfold), customers often find the crystal they intuitively choose without knowing anything about it (like me with astrophyllite). It is exactly what they need in that moment in time. Never ignore that little nudge or voice – it has your best intentions at heart.

While we do import and hand-choose an extensive number of crystals from our Australian suppliers, we also import from all over the world without touching or feeling them ourselves. We rely on photos, communication, trust and the ethical values of our sellers.

Connecting with crystals

A frequent question I get asked is, "Can I mix my crystals? Can my crystals sit next to each other on a shelf?" Truthfully, there is no right or wrong answer. It comes down to your personal preference, how you respond to crystal energy, and the energy that flows within your home.

I realise there are countless articles, predominantly on the internet, with recommendations of what you can and can't do with crystals, but I never pay attention to them. Why? Because, just like crystals, we are unique individuals who have a distinct energy vibration. What works for me may not work for you, and vice versa. I base my guidance and recommendations on the knowledge gained during my studies, all my years of working with crystals, healing others and, of course, what I've found works best for me.

My advice is, once you have formed a connection to your crystals and understand how each energy affects your

emotions and wellbeing, wear however many crystals you want. If you layer them all on without knowing their effect on you, this may leave you feeling jittery, overwhelmed and even nauseated. I learnt this early on in my course and through personal experience.

These days, I layer on at least 4 crystal healing bracelets daily, alongside my beloved turquoise, which basically never comes off! If a crystal energy doesn't resonate with me, I remove it and change the mix I'm wearing. It all comes down to tuning in to your intuition and finding what feels best for you.

As my daughter Taylar and I were having coffee one day, she reminded me that crystals will often have a different energy feeling (sensation) on different sides and parts of the body. At the time, Taylar was wearing a carnelian ring and had to swap it from her left finger to her right one, and immediately the energy evened out for her.

I have also experienced this phenomenon, where I have to take a crystal off within 5 minutes of wearing it. I feel sometimes we just don't need the extra energy, or perhaps our physical, emotional and mental wellbeing needs a different crystal entirely.

When placing crystals around your home, you will discover that some will resonate more strongly than others and be suited to certain rooms. Place them in a few places to begin with, and soon enough they will make it known to you where they want to reside. And, yes, they will communicate with you once you tune in to their frequency.

For example, when you've formed a connection and tuned in to your crystals, you may begin to feel their energy tingling in your palms when holding them; they may feel hot or cold, some may even drip water, and others will give you goosebumps or energy boosts.

If you are just beginning on your crystal journey, don't stress or compare your journey to others as I know it can seem overwhelming with so many things to remember. Focus on taking baby steps and work with one crystal for at least 5 days (if you can) as this will help you understand how the energy affects you. Once you spend time connecting and working with one crystal, you can then introduce another to the mix without becoming confused by the vibrations and feelings of each crystal.

Disappearing crystals

I must touch on crystal mishaps and disappearances!

As you have just learnt, every crystal has a unique energy vibration, just like we do. They have ancient wisdom and

 Walk in Beauty

healing properties from Mother Nature stored deep within their structure during growth. So, it makes sense that crystals can change their colour, energy and even their location.

Believe it or not (I know many people believe it's an impossibility, but I know for a fact), crystals can disappear. I've had it happen to me on a few occasions and other customers have encountered the same thing. I've received numerous emails and messages on our social media platforms from customers who become alarmed or think a curse has been placed upon them and that is why their crystals have moved locations or position overnight. Rest assured, if you ever experience this strange phenomenon, you are not cursed and there is nothing sinister involved.

Crystals can spontaneously disappear into thin air! As I said, I've had this happen a few times over the years. Some have returned to me, while others have moved on elsewhere. Where that mystery place is ... I truly don't know!

Another odd thing crystals can do is change colour and, ever so slightly, their shape. I'm not talking about crystals fading in the sun, which is completely normal; rather, I'm referring to crystals that fade in colour when you work with them. I've changed green jade eggs into white jade after using them for weeks in a spiritual practice, and, yes, they were 100% genuine green jade. I believe crystals change colour depending on our energy, how we use them, what we use them for and the energies they absorb on a daily basis.

Crystals can also move. I have never forgotten to this day when I was at home and had a beautiful clear quartz egg with the most amazing rainbow inclusions within him. He resided on a high hanging display shelf. I was walking past (nowhere near the crystal itself) and, right before my eyes, it jumped off the shelf and smashed at my feet. There was no wind, the shelves were secure and there were no vibrations or anything to move him. I was glad Ashley was there with me at the time because she witnessed it. Safe to say, I was heartbroken as this was my beloved crystal egg that I had formed a strong attachment to.

However, what we need to realise is that sometimes crystals need to move on, and they may even be dramatic when the time comes, especially if we don't recognise or sense the shift in their energy beforehand. I thanked my clear quartz egg for all his work and white-light energy and returned him to Mother Earth in the garden. Our garden is a haven for fairies and birds with all the sparkly crystals scattered among the plants, soil and trees.

 Walk in Beauty

If you feel any of your crystals no longer resonate with you, or if they disappear or fade in colour, interpret this as a positive sign that you have worked with the crystal energy for long enough, and it has offered you all the healing, protection and metaphysical benefits you needed up until this point.

You may choose to relocate your crystal as you begin working with a new crystal energy, or you may place it outside in nature if you feel your time together has come to an end. Perhaps gift it to another like-minded friend. Please, never discard crystals in the rubbish if they break because they are not trash – always return them to Mother Earth, if you can.

Remember, your crystal journey is never-ending, so allow yourself to be open to new crystal energies, shapes and healing properties because every stage of your life requires different healing, knowledge, teachings and energy.

The Sun God

We believe that the Sun God is all powerful,
for every Spring he makes the trees to bud
and the grass to grow.
We see these things with our own eyes,
and therefore we know that all life comes from him.

Anonymous. Blackfoot.

Walk in Beauty

Chapter 2

Crystal shapes

Depending on the type of healing you're seeking or the energy you wish to invoke and manifest, crystal shapes and carvings can influence how you feel and the ability to manifest what you want to achieve. Crystals differ in energy and metaphysical abilities, so when you choose the right one for whatever spiritual work you may be doing, it will make all the difference.

I've included a list of our most popular crystal shapes and forms and how they can help you in your spiritual journey.

Clusters and geodes

Crystal clusters and geodes are a favourite of mine because they can transform any negative energy into a lighter and positive feeling. Clusters contain integrated energies and are wonderful for any room of your home. They are a little family of terminations (crystal points and clusters) that bounce energy back and forth between each other and into your surrounds.

Crystal clusters and geodes are wonderful for:

- ☾ energising the atmosphere surrounding you with grounding and positive vibes
- ☾ using during crystal healing sessions, absent energy healing and distant Reiki sessions
- ☾ restoring a harmonious flow of energy to your body and wellbeing
- ☾ cleansing and charging smaller crystals and jewellery when placed near or on a crystal cluster.

Tips:

- ☾ Place an amethyst cluster beside your bed for peaceful sleep each night.
- ☾ Place a citrine cluster in your workspace or office to attract abundance.

Spheres

Crystal spheres are just so magickal to gaze into with their beautiful patterns. They promote/invoke peaceful, flowing energy into our surrounds, and it's for this reason I have many spheres placed throughout our home. They have a

gentle and soothing energy vibration, which makes them relaxing to hold in your palms.

If you're always on the go and find your mind is always switched on; for example, thinking about what to cook for dinner, what needs to be cleaned in the house, what you need to buy at the grocery shop ... crystal spheres are wonderful focal points to use during meditation and mindful-based practices.

It took me a long time to become good at meditation, and I found working with crystal spheres to be an essential asset.

Crystal spheres are wonderful for:

- ☾ using as a focal point during meditation practice
- ☾ incorporating during crystal healing to allow the body to receive even-flowing energy to the areas or ailments that need it most
- ☾ using for relaxation and sleep by placing a sphere by your bedside.

Tip:

If you have an overactive or wandering mind, gaze into a sphere and the energy will naturally help to clear your mind so you can concentrate on the present moment.

Crystal eggs

Crystal eggs are symbolic of fertility, creativity, good luck and abundance in all aspects of our life. Now, when I speak of fertility, I mean this in every sense, not just in pregnancy but in all areas of life, such as love, new beginnings, career ventures, happiness and contentment.

Crystal eggs are wonderful for:

- ☾ metaphysically healing – moving energy blocks and helping chronic pain areas
- ☾ locating blockages in your energy fields
- ☾ drawing pain out and away from your body using the pointed smaller end of your egg
- ☾ invoking harmonious energy into our wellbeing when holding a crystal egg during meditation.

Tip:

In healings such as Reiki and reflexology, crystal eggs are deeply relaxing to gently glide over the body, especially for foot massages (I love reflexology with crystals).

Walk in Beauty

Crystal hearts

Crystal hearts make a beautiful, heartfelt gift for a loved one. They hold a part of your energy and intention within them, and that in itself is magick. Crystal hearts share the energy of self-love, unconditional love, romantic love and universal love.

Crystal hearts will activate and open the heart chakra during a healing session. This process allows healing and loving energy to pass through you, and also helps to release any trauma, past hurts or heartbreaks.

Crystal hearts are wonderful for:
- ☾ attracting love and manifesting your true love (soul mate)
- ☾ gifting to loved ones, friends, family and pets
- ☾ being a comforting energy to carry with you in times of grief and loss
- ☾ having a calming and loving energy that can be utilised when connecting with the spirit world, e.g., passed loved ones, ancestors, angels, spirit guides and animals.

Generators, points, towers and double points

Crystal generators, points, towers and double points carry such an amazing power within their forms and are perfect energy boosters for both humans and other smaller crystals. They are symbolic of strength and teach us to be proud, stand tall and never give up when challenges arise in our path. Just like mountains, these crystal formations remind us to keep our foundations strong, stable and anchored to Mother Earth.

Crystal generators, points, towers and double points are wonderful for:

- ☾ connecting with higher spiritual energies and increasing psychic awareness
- ☾ offering protection and grounding during meditation and mindful-based practices
- ☾ placing around your home or business to attract prosperity, vitality and power
- ☾ using as a centrepiece in crystal grids to charge other crystals
- ☾ using when you or your crystals need a boost of energy and motivation.

 Walk in Beauty

Crystal wands

Crystal healing wands come in a variety of shapes, sizes and textures. Choosing a wand is a personal decision that will reflect what you intend to use it for and the type of energy you wish to manifest with it. Certain wands will feature double points that bring powerful healing as the energy is transmitted through both sides of the wand during a healing or meditation session. Other wands may be more rounded on the edges for all-over body healing.

Crystal wands are wonderful for:

- ☾ drawing excess energy out of your body using the widest point of the wand facing towards your body
- ☾ directing positive energy inward to your body using the smaller rounded end facing towards your body
- ☾ all-over body massages as wands help to relieve tension and ease and move knots in muscles
- ☾ touching each chakra to instil energy flow and positivity into your body during a crystal healing session.

Natural crystals

Natural crystals are unpolished, untreated, not carved and retain a unique energy and feeling of Mother Earth and her natural beauty. I just love natural crystals because they are beautiful to hold and work with. It all comes down to personal preference regarding whether you choose polished crystals or natural forms ... Remember, there is no right or wrong!

For me, I find natural crystals have a gentler energy than their polished-form friends. However, I know others who feel the opposite. One of my most-loved raw natural stones is calcite (in any colour) because it has a beautiful waxy, smooth surface and is just amazing to hold.

Natural crystals are wonderful for:

- ☾ using as décor or statement pieces in your home
- ☾ placing around your home to provide a natural energy boost and leave your space feeling grounded and peaceful
- ☾ healing sessions, when they can be placed on and around the body for a gentler healing energy.

Natural crystals may not sound as powerful energy-wise when compared to polished shapes and forms; however, their natural healing vibration is perfect for anyone who

experiences overwhelming or intense effects when working with polished crystals. You could argue that natural crystals have a deeper connection with Mother Earth, fairies and land guardians because their natural energy and formation remains undisturbed.

Tumble stones

I recommend these little forms to everyone, beginner and expert alike. Tumble stones are easy to get, are cost effective and are one of the best ways to work with new crystal energy. These little stones are polished smooth, making them ideal to carry with you anywhere, such as in your handbag, purse, bra and pockets.

This makes them a convenient way to receive crystal energy when you're on the go and can't carry a large crystal with you. Not to mention that tumble stones are a fantastic way to work with certain crystal types that are normally expensive, fragile or unattainable in a larger size.

Tumble stones are wonderful for:

- ☾ placing in your pillowcase or on your beside table for healing energy while you sleep
- ☾ placing near or on your phone, tablet and laptop for EMF protection

- ☾ placing in pot plants or among your garden plants to boost their health, harvest and growth
- ☾ placing in your car for safe travels (I've created a tumble stone pouch for this)
- ☾ wearing or carrying as a great way to receive crystal healing daily.

I'm also here to bust the myth that bigger is better. Nothing is further from the truth when it comes to crystals, and you also don't need to spend a fortune. The key to channelling and healing with crystal power is to always cleanse, charge and program them (I explain this mantra in Chapter 3).

So, never overlook the humble tumble. I love these little stones and over the past several years have collected hundreds, which all live in a large driftwood bowl together.

Worry stones/thumb stones

These little forms are just as reliable as tumbles. They slip into your pocket or bra with ease, and they are a touch stone. Touch stones are crystal forms that you develop a deeper connection with the more you touch them. The more time you spend holding or using your worry/thumb stone, the more amplified the energy between you and the crystal becomes.

Worry/thumb stones are wonderful for:
- ☾ reducing stress, anxiety and needless worry
- ☾ raising the good endorphins in our bodies
- ☾ releasing tension from our wellbeing, which assists in relieving body aches
- ☾ helping to reduce blood pressure as they provide a calming effect on your body's nervous system.

If you suffer from high blood pressure due to daily stress and triggers, thumb/worry stones are wonderful to promote soothing vibes to your body, mind and emotions. I have "white coat hypertension" (yes, it's a legitimate stress response, look it up!), and whenever I visit the doctor for a routine script repeat, my breathing and heart rate become fast and uneven.

I have no idea why it happens as my doctor is awesome, but I always wear a lapis lazuli healing bracelet when I visit, for this reason. We have a laugh most times he takes my blood pressure as some readings come back normal and other times he nearly falls off his chair!

Coloured crystals and aura quartz

An abundance of controversy surrounds these types of crystals. Why, I don't quite understand. They are real crystals that have been enhanced by adding a splash of colour, extra minerals or other precious metals to their outer layer. The extra properties used to amplify the colours and vibrational energy of natural crystals enhance and reflect an extension of the crystal's natural beauty within.

Not to mention that their vibrant tones naturally assist in uplifting our emotions, boosting our mood and reminding us that decorating our space with colourful décor is an easy yet powerful way to brighten the energy in our atmosphere. I personally love working with this crystal energy.

Another important fact about coloured crystals and aura quartz is the ethical and zero-waste process behind them. Often, aura quartz and coloured agate will contain small surface imperfections that occur during the growth phase of the crystal. However, crystal suppliers no longer automatically discard crystals as waste if they are an odd shape or colour; instead, they have found a way to enhance and utilise every part of the crystal.

This is commendable because any crystal is a gift from Earth and deserves to be cherished. In my opinion, anyone who wants "perfect" crystals doesn't truly appreciate the crystal world and the healing benefits that all crystal forms, shapes and colours have to offer us. But

 Walk in Beauty

this is simply my perspective, and we can always agree to disagree.

However, I do encourage anyone who is embarking on their crystal and spiritual journey to do their research, have an open mind, work with various crystals – natural, rough, polished, mixed crystal energy – as you may just change your view on the heightened energy that aura quartz and agate have to share with you.

If you're still not convinced, think about colour-enhanced crystals like this: when we wear makeup, eyelash extensions, dye our hair or wear hair extensions, paint our fingernails and adorn ourselves in accessories that reflect our persona, we are still the same person underneath.

Our unique energy remains the same because our spiritual vibration cannot be completely altered or changed by adding things on a surface level. What we may experience, however, is a boost in our self-confidence, happiness and energy vibration that stems from feeling beautiful as we wear what brings us joy. So, once again, we are not fake for enhancing our natural beauty and neither are colour- and mineral-enhanced crystals.

Aura quartz crystals are wonderful for:
- ☾ uplifting our emotional and mental states in a positive way
- ☾ increasing energy levels and cleansing our auric field and chakras
- ☾ receiving a naturally generated, magnified energy vibration
- ☾ colour (therapy) healing for our wellbeing by connecting and working with the colourful rays of happiness and energy.

 Walk in Beauty

Our Earth

The old Indian teaching was that it is wrong to tear loose from its place on Earth anything that may be growing there. It may be cut off, but it should not be uprooted. The trees and the grass have spirits. Whenever one of such growths may be destroyed by some good Indian, his act is done in sadness and with a prayer for forgiveness because of his necessities...

Wooden Leg, 1858–1940. Cheyenne.

Chapter 3

Cleanse, charge and program

My mantra is: *Cleanse. Charge. Program.* During my crystal studies, it was reiterated to us to "always" look after our crystals by keeping them open to the highest of "good and vibrating with positive and healing energy". However, over the years I've read many articles where certain healers believe that because crystals hold their own unique energy, they never require any cleansing maintenance before, during and after use. So, depending on what your intuition tells you, trust what works best for you because there is no right or wrong way.

Personally, I would never skip the steps below (cleanse, charge and program) because I feel a huge difference when I take the time to tend to my crystals. For example, if I haven't used a particular crystal in a while that has been sitting on my shelf, I often notice she may seem a little duller in energy than her friends, who have been used recently.

Walk in Beauty

By following my simple mantra, you will undoubtedly notice your crystals will be high-vibing 24/7 without any stagnant energy weighing down their natural healing properties. I have included an outline of my favourite crystal empowering techniques and other ways you may wish to try. Remember, it's about finding what feels right for you and your crystals.

Cleanse

White sage: I always use white sage smudge bundles with my abalone shell and feather to cleanse my crystals, jewellery, spiritual trinkets and home. White sage helps to remove negative energies, while lowering vibrations and instilling positive and fresh energy.

This beautiful herb is a traditional Native American approach, so, of course, being proud of my Cherokee heritage, I hold this smudging herb in the highest regard. Smudging, as it's named by Indigenous tribes, also allows you to bless your crystals and yourself during your ceremony, ritual or cleansing practice.

The advantage of using sage smoke is that it will never damage any crystal and will cleanse everything within your surrounds with pure and natural smoke. I've found smudging to be the easiest and safest method of them all. See Chapter 6 for an explanation of how to smudge.

Tibetan singing bowls: This is a wonderful method to cleanse your crystals using sound vibration because crystals adore sound frequency, and your plants will too. Smaller tumble stones may be placed inside the bowl while you play it, if you like. You will discover that the additional vibrations and movements of the stones will lead to an unusual vibration and sensation within your singing bowl.

Water: A lot of crystals don't like water, and it can cause damage to their structure and surface if they are immersed, even briefly. So please do your research prior to submerging any crystals in water. As a general rule, most crystals ending in "ite" are not fans of water, so please avoid this so you don't accidentally damage them.

Water (from lakes, creeks, rivers and the ocean) can be a beautiful way to clean your crystals, especially crystal clusters, which often accumulate dust within them. Take care using salt water as it can be abrasive, and always rinse with clean, fresh water.

Visualisation: Using your third eye chakra to visualise is an additional way to cleanse your crystals and enhance your connection with your psychic abilities. To use the

visualisation method, simply hold your crystals in your palms and place them in line with your mind's eye (third eye). Concentrate on visualising positive white-light flowing energy surrounding your crystals. As you do this, you may sense heaviness or stagnant vibes being lifted from your crystals.

Mother Earth: Burying your crystals in Mother Earth (nature) overnight is a wonderful cleansing experience to try. By cleansing and charging your crystals in the earth, the grounding energy absorbed into your crystals is naturally transferred to you when working with your crystals, which is perfect for anyone who may have unbalanced emotions.

Ensure the soil is dry and lightly covers your crystal, or, alternatively, use potting mix or even pop your crystal into a pot plant. I have many crystals living in outdoor and indoor plants and find the combination to be a match made in heaven.

Charge

Now that we have removed all the heavy vibes from our crystals, let's infuse them with high vibes so that their energy is amplified and they're ready to work with.

Moonlight: Crystals love charging under the silvery glow of the full moon, or any lunar phase in all honesty. I love the new moon as the energy is not as strong or intense and encourages new beginnings, new paths and new uplifted energy, which is always a good thing!

You may choose to leave your crystals outside in a safe place or inside your window, where they can receive moonlight. This is my preference because otherwise it would take me a couple of days to move all my crystals outside, and who has time to do that?

Sunlight and warmth: Sunlight from Father Sun is a beautiful cleansing/charging method as the sun naturally produces life-bringing and positive energy. However, you need to be mindful to not leave your crystals in direct hot sun for prolonged periods of time as this can lead to them fading in colour.

I love the morning sun or the afternoon golden hour because the sunlight is gentle with lower UV levels, which will not hinder your crystals' energy. I keep many of my crystals outdoors as I don't mind a lighter shade of amethyst, rose quartz, calcite or agate, to be honest.

Crystal energy: Crystals charging crystals? Absolutely! The best crystals for charging other stones are amethyst,

 Walk in Beauty

citrine, clear quartz and selenite. Amethyst and citrine clusters will naturally amplify the vibration of smaller crystals when placed beside them. Alternatively, charge your crystals directly by placing them on your amethyst or citrine clusters.

Clear quartz generators work similarly to a battery recharge for your smaller crystals. Placing your smaller crystals in a circle around a clear quartz generator will naturally enhance and transfer the pure white-light energy that radiates from quartz onto your other crystals.

I've found that quartz is often underrated when compared to exotically named crystals, and many people consider it boring. I struggle to understand this because nothing is further from the truth. Quartz is an absolute must-have crystal for everyone!

Selenite generators or charging plates are brilliant charging methods because selenite resonates with moonlight, cleanses our aura and is a high-vibration yet gentle cleansing crystal energy to work with.

Charging plates do exactly what they sound like – they naturally charge your crystals when they are placed on top of the selenite plate. You can even place your drink (your glass of moon water) on them, but just ensure you don't accidentally wet selenite because she doesn't like water.

Program

Crystals need us to tell them what healing or energy we require from them, otherwise they remain a beautiful-looking stone without truly sharing their full metaphysical potential with us.

To program your crystal with a clear intention, hold it in your palms and place it in front of your third eye chakra (mid-forehead and between the brows). With a relaxed mind and clear intention, speak to your crystal (aloud or silently because both ways effectively program your crystal) and relay your wishes, manifestation or intention.

The key is to keep it simple and precise and avoid rambling with too many details or instructions because this will not work for you or your crystal. Also, I recommend programming one crystal at a time, with the exception of our healing pouches, as the crystals chosen for pouches are based on their ability to work together with a clear intention and harmonious energy.

When you program your crystals, you may wish for good health and healing, inner balance, abundance and success, happiness, love, harmony, prosperity, courage, etc. Just make sure you use the appropriate crystal that aligns with your desired outcomes and energy because this makes manifesting and programming more successful.

Walk in Beauty

Use your third eye to visualise (or imagine if you're still developing your psychic abilities) an image of your desired outcome or intention you are asking your crystal to help with. Envision your dream as something that is already playing out in the future (imagine it as a short reel/movie).

The more you manifest and plant the seeds of your dreams into the universe, the more amplified the intention becomes. Lastly, always give thanks to your crystals and the universe for the healing vibrations and energy they have shared with you.

Congratulations! You have just put forth your best energy and dreams into action by following these easy steps.

Your Path

Everything is laid out for you.
Your path is straight ahead of you.
Sometimes it's invisible but it's there.
You may not know where it's going,
but you have to follow that path.
It's the path to the Creator.
It's the only path there is.

Chief Leon Shenandoah, 1990. Onondaga.

Walk in Beauty

Chapter 4

Chakras, auras and crystals

Crystals benefit our spiritual and physical wellbeing in every possible way. Their metaphysical energy connects with our chakras and spiritual bodies, which surround our physical body. We may not consciously see our spiritual bodies or psychic energy, but on a daily basis we can connect and channel this energy in an unconscious way.

Spiritual aura

Aura is a word we hear and read about everywhere in Eastern philosophy when it comes to healing and spiritual practices, but what actually is it? Put simply, our aura radiates colours depending on our current energy, health, emotional and mental wellbeing.

Depending on the country you live in and the spiritual mentors or practices you follow, you may also hear aura being referred to as energy bodies. The terminology is used interchangeably and both phrases share the same metaphysical meaning.

Like all spiritual bodies, our aura surrounds our physical body like a protective shield against psychic vampires and low-vibrating energy. The colours our aura reflects are an accurate indication of our authentic self. Our aura may change colour often depending on our life circumstances, personality and health, and the size of auras may also expand or diminish depending on the state of our wellbeing. Depending on our spiritual and psychic gifts, certain people can see or feel the aura of those surrounding them.

During a Reiki session with a client (I refer to myself as being in the "Reiki zone"), I can sometimes glimpse their aura colour as I concentrate on connecting with their energy, and other times I will hear it spoken from a higher spiritual guide.

This ability has taken me countless years of practising and regular meditation to develop. I honestly can't explain how I initially started seeing and hearing aura colours, but it appears my spiritual gifts continue to develop and evolve as I do my weekly Reiki healings.

Something I absolutely love that occurs during or after a Reiki healing for clients is that their auric energy transitions

into a beautiful bright-blue glowing light. This colour reflects the harmonious and peaceful energy that was passed on to your aura, chakras and wellbeing during the Reiki healing.

Did you know, when the physical body dies, our aura departs completely and our spirit transcends into the next world so our soul can return home again.

The etheric body

Our etheric body connects with our mind and nervous system, and we use crystals to alleviate and clear trapped energy in our etheric form, which is often seen as a fine grey mist that surrounds our physical body.

Crystals connect strongly with this level of our body's vibration and help to remove any blocked energy before it can manifest into dis-ease or physical illness. By integrating crystal healing into youro self-care practices, your etheric body and nervous system will naturally experience an increase of flowing harmonious energy.

The physical body

Our physical body has several more layers than our spiritual bodies and is considered denser in energy when compared to the lighter metaphysical energies that surround us. Our physical body is prone to developing aches, pains and ailments that may stem from emotional, mental or spiritual imbalance.

Throughout our lifetime, we may experience a sense of disconnection to nature and spirit, and feel as though the weight of the world is on our shoulders. When these feelings arise, it symbolises that our metaphysical and physical bodies are misaligned with blocked energy. By connecting with Mother Earth and spending time in nature, we absorb negative ions that naturally boost our immunity, wellbeing and outlook on life.

The mental body

Our mental body extends from our astral body and hovers close to several feet around our physical body at any given time. Our mental body mirrors our daily emotions, thoughts and subconscious patterns.

During Reiki healing, I clear the person's mental body because we often harbour lingering feelings of anger, fear, greed, negativity or jealousy when the energy becomes blocked. Once the energy is cleared, they will experience an increase in positive feelings of love, joy, compassion, purity and happiness.

Chakras

Chakras are an energy system we focus on when we wish to heal our body using either crystals or alternate energy healing like Reiki, sound clearing, crystal healing and kinesiology.

Working with our chakras can assist us in reaching a deeper meditative and grounded state, increase our energy levels, enrich relationships, balance our emotions, develop empathy for those around us, develop clearer and honest communication ... the list goes on!

Each of our main 7 chakras resonate with a specific colour and crystal energy. It is up to you which crystals you choose to work with. In most cases, the crystal aligns with the colour and energy of the chakra you are working with.

Below, I have included an easy-to-follow guide to help you on your crystal and chakra journey.

Root chakra

Colour connection: Red or black.

Key purpose: Our foundation and connection to Mother Earth.

Crystal choice: Choose crystals that are deep and opaque in tone, e.g., black obsidian, black tourmaline, garnet, ruby or jaspers.

Overview: Our root chakra is located at the base of our spine and provides us with stability in our metaphysical and physical body. Many people wish to ascend to a higher spiritual level but, sadly, most are not willing to ground or channel the energy in their root chakra.

When this chakra is blocked, you may notice your head feels like it's in the clouds, or you have a lack of mental focus, unbalanced emotions and a state of rigidity that stems from not going with the flow.

Mantra:

*I ask for connectedness with Mother Earth
to keep my roots strong and nurtured.*

Sacral chakra

Colour connection: Orange.

Key purpose: Our sexuality, creativity and emotional energy.

 Walk in Beauty

Crystal choice: Choose crystals that ignite feminine and goddess energy, e.g., orange calcite, bloodstone, carnelian, peach moonstone, or mookaite.

Overview: Our sacral chakra is located below the navel (groin region) and encompasses our life force, ambition and creative energy. To keep your sacral chakra balanced and full of vitality, choose crystals that promote fertility, sensuality and self-expression.

When your sacral chakra is flowing with positive energy, you will find your relationships with others will be positive and passionate as your inner flame will burn bright.

When this chakra is blocked, you will experience a lack of motivation, inspiration and enthusiasm for life.

Mantra:

*I call upon Goddess Isis for creativity, fertility
in all areas, and passion for life.*

Solar plexus chakra

Colour connection: Yellow.

Key purpose: Our connection to Father Sun, empowerment and inner strength.

Crystal choice: Choose crystals that have golden and warm tones, e.g., amber, citrine, topaz, tiger's eye, or jaspers.

Overview: Our solar plexus chakra is located in the stomach region and provides us with core support, strength and resilience. This chakra is responsible for our happiness, confidence, outlook on life and our daily drive to complete the tasks set out before us.

When this chakra is blocked, we may feel sluggish, experience digestive issues, lack self-confidence and struggle to see the positivity around us.

Mantra:

*I open myself up to abundance, health
and positivity from Father Sun.*

Heart chakra

Colour connection: Green or pink.

Key purpose: Our connection to our inner centre, emotions, empathy and understanding.

Crystal choice: Choose crystals that have pink or green tones, e.g., rose quartz, rhodonite, malachite, green aventurine, or pink opal.

 Walk in Beauty

Overview: Our heart chakra is located in the centre of our chest. This chakra radiates loving, nurturing, compassion and gentle energy that flows within and out of our being. Our heart chakra allows for relationships to grow, for us to feel empathy for others, find balance within ourselves, and, most of all, encourages us to love our authentic self.

When this chakra is blocked, we may have feelings of isolation, lack emotional connection, be critical of others and feel no self-love within ourselves.

Mantra:

*Every day is my time to flourish, grow
and open my heart to universal love.*

Throat chakra

Colour connection: Blue.

Key purpose: Our ability to use our voice, speak our truth and communicate with others.

Crystal choice: Choose crystals in pale- or dark-blue tones, e.g., blue kyanite, lapis lazuli, blue calcite, blue lace agate, or turquoise.

Overview: Our throat chakra is located in the centre of our neck (throat). This chakra affects how we interact and communicate with others in daily life. When our throat chakra is open and flowing with energy, you will communicate clearly with others, be filled with clarity, positive thinking and enthusiasm for life.

When this chakra is blocked, you may find yourself repressing the things you need to say, lacking in motivation and feeling lost within yourself and the world.

Mantra:

I speak my truth and embrace my authentic self.

Third eye chakra

Colour connection: Indigo or purple.

Key purpose: Our connection to higher realms, spirituality, purity and mysticism.

Crystal choice: Choose crystals in deep blue and purple tones, e.g., sodalite, sapphire, iolite, amethyst, or purple fluorite.

Overview: Our third eye chakra is located in the centre of our forehead (between the brows). This chakra is an

exciting one as it's for all things spiritual. Our third eye (mind's eye) allows us to awaken and channel our inner knowing and intuitive knowledge that we carry within our soul in every lifetime we live.

By practising divination and meditation regularly, you naturally strengthen your connection to your third eye, which allows for spiritual growth and exploration in the higher realms, astral planes, and for magick to emerge over time.

When this chakra is blocked, you may lack seeing the signs and blessings surrounding you. Your mind will lack clarity as it is overburdened with needless chatter. You may also suffer stress headaches and a lack of focus.

Mantra:

*I am a mystical being and I open
my intuition to higher knowledge.*

Crown chakra

Colour connection: Violet or clear.

Key purpose: Our connection to enlightenment, inner peace and spiritual protection.

Crystal choice: Choose crystals in violet or translucent tones, e.g., clear quartz, lemurian seed, hackmanite, optical calcite, or apophyllite.

Overview: Our crown chakra is located at the top of our head. This chakra is our connection to the universe and all it has to offer, and allows for personal and spiritual growth to emerge.

When your crown chakra is clear and open it is symbolic of unlocking a door into the vast cosmos and drinking in all her ancient knowledge and teachings. We connect with higher realms, expand our mind to new possibilities, and are always protected by the highest of white-light healing energy when working with this chakra.

Our crown chakra is deeply connected to our root chakra as we cannot ascend higher without first being grounded and connected to Mother Earth. When this chakra is blocked, you may needlessly worry, feel like you are at a standstill in life, and struggle to move forward due to a lack of self-awareness.

Mantra:

*Enlightenment and blessings
surround me from the Creator.*

 Walk in Beauty

Colour therapy

Now that we've delved into spiritual bodies and chakras, let's explore the power of colour therapy and crystals. If you're just starting out on your spiritual journey and have limited crystals to work with, rest assured that colour therapy – wearing colours in the form of makeup, hair colour, clothes and jewellery, decorating rooms in your house with various colours, the colours you eat, etc. – are all subtle yet powerful ways to heal, uplift and ground your space.

When you think of a rainbow it usually makes you smile. I'm in awe of Mother Nature, and she reminds me that there is always a light at the end of any storm or dark day I may be experiencing.

Colours have an impact on our daily life without us even realising. Our emotions, mindset, health and even our productivity can be influenced by the colours that surround us. I'm going to share a little insight into how you can incorporate colour therapy into your daily routine and spiritual practices to maximise your wellbeing using crystals or colours in general.

You may be seeking an increase in energy and vitality, or perhaps the total opposite if you're craving rest and peaceful sleep. The wonderful thing about colour therapy is that there is a colour for everything we need. It's just a matter of learning how certain colours affect us and making the conscious effort to integrate more colours into our lives.

Just as our chakras resonate with certain colours, our crystals have unique healing properties that connect with us in different ways, which is why you never truly rely on one crystal for all of your needs.

What many people don't realise is that you can heal yourself with crystals based purely on the colour you feel drawn to. It really can be that easy. Below is a general guide to colour therapy, so whether you're using crystals, décor or accessories for colour therapy, this guide will help you in your colour journey.

Red:

- ☾ For renewal of our energy and vitality.
- ☾ For promoting sensuality, passion and love.
- ☾ Grounding and balancing for our physical body.
- ☾ Beneficial if you experience lethargy, lack in motivation and feel detached from life.

 Walk in Beauty

Orange:
- ☾ Can promote optimism, joy and happiness.
- ☾ Releases stagnant energy blocks from our spiritual bodies and raises our vibration.
- ☾ Good for boosting our immunity.
- ☾ Wonderful for increasing creativity, uplifting our mood and releasing sadness.

Yellow:
- ☾ Soothes our nervous system and relaxes our body.
- ☾ Shares wisdom as it releases feelings of negativity.
- ☾ Signifies life-giving energy, joy and happiness.
- ☾ Perfect for cleansing our wellbeing and boosting feelings of self-worth, confidence and humour.

Green:
- ☾ For connecting with Mother Nature and nature spirits.
- ☾ Promotes harmony and healing in relationships.
- ☾ Encourages us to embrace new beginnings, relationships and experiences.
- ☾ Beautiful for welcoming unconditional love and nurturing energy into our life.

Blue:
- ☾ Promotes trust, honesty and open communication.
- ☾ Delivers a peaceful and cooling effect on our spiritual and physical bodies.
- ☾ Relaxes our mind and may lower blood pressure.
- ☾ Deeply healing, while sharing feelings of calmness, composure and self-control.

Indigo:
- ☾ Useful for meditation, spiritual wisdom and purification.
- ☾ Encourages us to never give up on our dreams, and sparks inspiration.
- ☾ Symbolic of a starry night, universal planes and the unconscious mind.
- ☾ Wonderful to use when embarking on a new career venture and manifesting new beginnings.

White:
- ☾ Promotes creativity, intuition, purity and growth.
- ☾ Spiritual and protective white-light energy offers healing and renewal.
- ☾ Helps release emotional baggage and assists in breaking addictions and obsessive behaviours.

- ☾ Encourages feelings of hope, creativity, inspiration and positive energy.
- ☾ Wonderful for clearing negative energy and blocks from our system so we can welcome positive healing and harmony into our life and self.

Grey:

- ☾ Promotes neutrality, balance and calmness.
- ☾ Symbolic of a crossroads in our journey and what to do next.
- ☾ Soothing for the mind and emotions.
- ☾ A reminder to approach things gently and conservatively.
- ☾ Guides us to see the "grey" in situations rather than seeing things as black or white.

Purple:

- ☾ A mystical, spiritual and creative colour.
- ☾ For developing a deeper understanding and awareness of the universe.
- ☾ Awakens our psychic centres and enhances our intuition.
- ☾ Brings protective and harmonious energy to our surrounds and self.
- ☾ Attracts all the magick from the universe.

Black:
- ☾ Symbolises elegance, protection and mysterious energy.
- ☾ Boosts our self-confidence and esteem.
- ☾ Healing for feelings of grief and melancholy.
- ☾ Provides comfort when feelings of loneliness and melancholy arise.

Pink:
- ☾ The colour of universal love and emotional wellbeing.
- ☾ For attracting genuine friendships.
- ☾ Can help you open yourself up to attracting love and kindness into your life.
- ☾ For connecting with your inner child and playful energy.
- ☾ Encourages feelings of harmony, inner peace and hope.

Brown:
- ☾ A colour for grounding and connection to nature.
- ☾ Brings balance and stability to your body and wellbeing.
- ☾ Encourages feelings of security and warmth.
- ☾ Induces relaxation and increases serotonin for your mindset, sleep and immunity.

 Walk in Beauty

Our Earth

Everything on Earth has a purpose,
Every disease and herb to cure it,
And every person a mission.
This is the Indian theory of existence.

Mourning Dove, 1888–1936. Coast Salish.

Chapter 5

Healing everyday ailments with crystals

Tumble stones are ideal for healing our daily ailments, including headaches, anxiety and stress levels, and for promoting hormonal balance, self-love, sleep and calming emotions. They are lightweight and smooth for placing on the body, affordably priced, and there is an extensive number to choose from. I love creating little crystal healing pouches for our website as they simplify the process of choosing the crystals beneficial for your ailment or issue.

I'm going to share our top 10 most-loved pouches, the combination of crystals used, and briefly explain how their energies work together to help your concern. This section may also serve as a crystal reference guide for you, especially if you already have certain crystals in your collection and didn't realise how they can work together to help you in your daily life.

 Walk in Beauty

You will find full crystal pouch descriptions and metaphysical information about every individual crystal on our *MoonstoneGypsyAU* website. If I included every little detail in this chapter about our pouches and crystals, I would have to start another book!

I recommend placing any of the crystals mentioned below on your body for direct-skin contact. Alternatively, place one crystal in your bra or pocket, or place a crystal pouch in your handbag if you want to carry your crystals around with you all the time. You can also place your crystal pouch beside your bed at night or in your pillowcase to absorb the healing, nurturing and soothing crystal energy as you sleep.

Begin your crystal healing at home by following these steps:

Step 1.   Clear your crystals of energy so they are a blank canvas of pure vibrations.

Step 2.   Hold all your crystals in your palms if they are being used together, or choose 1 or 2 crystals. Gently hold your crystals to your third eye and speak in simple terms (aloud or silently), outlining what you wish to achieve from your crystal healing, such as healing a headache, attracting good luck, clearing your mind of wandering thoughts. The trick is to not ramble too much when setting your intention.

Step 3. Place your crystals on your body where they coincide with the chakras you wish to heal or balance. If you find the crystals fall off, simply cradle them in your palms or place them on the outer edge of your physical body as this will allow them to connect with your spiritual bodies.

Step 4. Allow yourself to relax for 10 to 20 minutes, if possible. If you are feeling sleepy after your crystal healing, treat yourself to a well-deserved nap!

Step 5. Once you've completed your healing, remove your crystals and remember to thank them. Always cleanse your crystals after any healings you do, or after wearing and carrying them all day, as this will help remove any stagnant or negative energy they have absorbed for you. I always individually cleanse each crystal after use to ensure they are thoroughly cleared.

Remember the mantra I gave you back in Chapter 3? *Cleanse. Charge. Program.* Follow those wonderful steps. But, for now, let's get back to our most-loved crystal pouches and how they can help you.

 Walk in Beauty

Anxiety and panic pouch

Purpose: Soothing for our mind and emotions and invoking feelings of inner calm and peace.

Chakra connection: Root, heart and third eye chakras.

Crystal combination:

- ☾ Green aventurine – Mother Nature healing and grounding.
- ☾ Sodalite – connecting and calming our mind and emotions.
- ☾ Tiger's eye – invokes inner strength, resilience and courage.
- ☾ Amethyst – releases stress and anxiety and clears negative energy.

Mantra:

I open myself to calm and peace.
I release worry into the universe to
dissipate in the winds of change, A'ho.

Attracting abundance pouch

Purpose: Using high vibrations to attract positivity and abundance into our life.

Chakra connection: Sacral, heart and crown chakras.

Crystal combination:

- ☾ Smoky quartz – acts as a shield of protection against low-vibrating energy.
- ☾ Tree agate – strengthens our relationships and supports self-growth.
- ☾ Orange calcite – attracts joy, abundance, happiness and vitality.
- ☾ Dalmatian jasper – brings balance while removing toxins and negativity.

Mantra:

*I am surrounded by abundance in every form;
my light shines bright from within, A'ho.*

Big love pouch

Purpose: Attract all kinds of love into your life while receiving nurturing and compassionate energy.

Chakra connection: Root, sacral, heart and crown chakras.

Crystal combination:

- ☾ Green aventurine – Mother Nature healing, grounding and positive wellbeing.

- ☾ Rose quartz – encourages unconditional love, self-respect and compassion.
- ☾ Rhodonite – balancing for yin–yang energy and helps release trauma.
- ☾ Lepidolite – increases mindfulness and positive new behaviours and discourages self-sabotaging patterns.

Mantra:

We are all connected upon Mother Earth,
so let us share and feel love every day;
my heart is open for connection, A'ho.

Cancer/chemo pouch

Purpose: I created this pouch to help those experiencing cancer and terminal illness, and their family going through the emotional struggle. The crystal energies work together to bring forth support, love, faith and to detoxify our emotions of negativity.

Chakra connection: Root, sacral, solar plexus and heart chakras.

Crystal combination:

- ☾ Snowflake obsidian – generates positive and balancing energy.

- ☾ Malachite – offers protection, love and transformation into a new phase.
- ☾ Sunstone – invokes positivity, joy and re-energising energy.
- ☾ Bloodstone – detoxes and removes toxins, and uplifts and improves circulation.

Mantra:

Illness does not define me;
I walk my path with determination,
protection from my ancestors,
and fresh new growth.
I am surrounded with healing blue rays and light, A'ho.

Chronic pain pouch

Purpose: I honestly can't remember a day without chronic pain! I know many of you will relate to this ailment. This targets various body pains and helps remove tension and aches.

Chakra connection: Sacral, heart and throat chakras.

Crystal combination:

- ☾ Sodalite – encourages sleep and soothes body aches.

 Walk in Beauty

- ☾ Selenite – cleanses our aura of stagnant energy for renewal.
- ☾ Red jasper – increases vitality, body circulation and balance.
- ☾ Amazonite – induces calming energy and removes energy blocks.

Mantra:

*I release all past trauma and pain.
I call in new energy and healing.
I cherish my body and rest as needed, A'ho.*

Fertility talisman pouch

Purpose: One of my favourite pouches that has supported many happy goddesses conceiving and delivering their babies. I know I cannot take credit, but I believe the crystal energies helped many women in their fertility journey by connecting with their body and mind.

Chakra connection: Sacral and heart chakras.

Crystal combination:

- ☾ Selenite – hormonal balancing and a fertility talisman.
- ☾ Unakite – wonderful for conception, pregnancy and birth.

- ☾ Carnelian – connecting with sexual health, fertility, vitality and goddess energy.
- ☾ Rainbow moonstone – invokes new beginnings, feminine energy, and balances our mood and emotions.

Mantra:

Fertility is mine within all areas of my life.
I am good and I attract good.
I flourish and bloom with Mother Nature, A'ho.

Grief easing pouch

Purpose: Grief is a time of roller-coaster emotions, heartbreak and loss that the majority of us will experience at least once in our lifetime. I dedicated this pouch to our beloved Whippet Bella after she passed as I needed crystal healing to help me through my grief. This assortment of crystals supports our emotional health and provides us with a sense of faith.

Chakra connection: Root, solar plexus and heart chakras.

Crystal combination:

- ☾ Apache tears – deeply healing for emotional trauma, sorrow and grief. These beautiful stones received

their name in honour of the Apache tribe in Arizona following their deaths after an incident on Apache Leap Mountain.

- ☾ Rose quartz – gentle nurturing energy for self-esteem, love, forgiveness and understanding.
- ☾ Dalmatian jasper – encourages happiness, joy and positivity.
- ☾ Sunstone – carries bright light rays to clear any negativity we may be holding within ourselves.
- ☾ Green aventurine – gentle healing energy that builds in power over time.

Mantra:

There are no goodbyes, for our soul never dies.
We have a change of worlds, until we meet again;
I cherish our memories, A'ho.

Hashimoto's/thyroid pouch

Purpose: Being diagnosed with an autoimmune disease changes your life. I created this to help myself on my health journey because supportive and calm energies are essential.

Chakra connection: Solar plexus, heart and throat chakras.

Crystal combination:
- ☾ Lapis lazuli – deeply easing for body inflammation.
- ☾ Dumortierite – encourages a positive and healthy outlook on life.
- ☾ Blue quartz – soothing for our thyroid and naturally boosts our immunity.
- ☾ New jade – supportive of hair health and hormonal balance.
- ☾ Citrine – boosts digestion and energy when lethargy is present.

Mantra:

*Every illness makes me aware of my capabilities.
My body deserves care, and I shall honour it
with the respect it deserves, A'ho.*

Headache/migraine pouch

Purpose: My husband suffers from a headache most days, despite trying countless remedies. This crystal combination works for stress, sinus and hormonal headaches by easing the blocked tension.

Chakra connection: Sacral, throat, third eye and crown chakras.

 Walk in Beauty

Crystal combination:

- ☾ Amethyst – removes stress and invokes relaxation and mindfulness.
- ☾ White howlite – diffuses anger, stress and negative energy that may be causing disharmony.
- ☾ Sodalite – easing for stress and anxiety and helps reduce inflammation in our body.
- ☾ Clear quartz – offers all-over healing from our head to toes, and encourages harmony and peaceful energy.

Mantra:

I still my mind and bring balance to both sides.
Harmony is always within my reach.
I release anything that does not bring clarity, A'ho.

Insomnia/nightmares pouch

Purpose: Sleep renews our physical and mental wellbeing. The crystal energy of this pouch helps us feel relaxed, invokes deeper sleep and encourages feelings of security.

Chakra connection: Sacral, third eye and throat chakras.

Crystal combination:
- ☾ Rainbow moonstone – encourages lucid dreaming and is calming for emotions.
- ☾ Labradorite – helps to clear your mind of worries and thoughts that may be keeping you awake.
- ☾ Angelite – connecting with guardian angels and providing peace of mind.
- ☾ Hematite – natural pain reliever, grounding for the mind and body, and provides a sense of security.

Mantra:

*I am surrounded by the love and
energy of my angels, guides and ancestors.
Sleep is my connection with them, and I will rest
soundly and find peace within my dreams, A'ho.*

 Walk in Beauty

The Earth

The Earth is your grandmother and mother, and she is sacred.
Every step that is taken upon her should be as a prayer.

Black Elk (Hehaka Sapa), 1863–1950. Ogala Lakota.

Chapter 6

Smudging with sacred herbs

When it comes to sage and any of the herb smudge sticks we sell, I always ensure we buy ethically grown and sustainable sage. Like with crystals, it is essential to do your research on whom you are choosing to purchase from.

You can always ask a business where their crystals, herbs and sage are sourced from, and if they are legit, they will have no reason not to provide you with this information. I include the origin of our items in the descriptions on our website and will happily answer any questions that people may have.

Now, before we continue, I need to touch on a particular notion about smudging ... There have been dozens of reels and written articles that deem the phrase "smudging" as offensive to use unless you are of an Indigenous ethnicity. The important thing to remember, like with any cultural

or spiritual practice and belief system, is that respect and consideration go a long way.

Providing you are mindful, grateful, respectful, and understand the sacred value of your spiritual practices and the herbs you are using, then you're doing right by the culture's traditions and honouring the ritualistic intent behind the spiritual tools or herbs.

However, I know there will be people who do not agree with me and that is perfectly fine. I have Cherokee blood and love everything my culture encompasses. I do not personally find it offensive when other cultures use smudging as a way of cleansing and clearing their space.

Sage

White sage is an ancient, natural herb that is favoured by various cultures and people. It is often used in ceremonies, sacred spaces and for prayers to spirit. Traditional healers, shamans and Native American cultures have used sage smudging as a cleansing and healing method for thousands of years.

I use sage in my morning routine as it allows me to send love, gratitude and blessings to my ancestors and passed loved ones in the billowing smoke. In return, they send guidance, love and protection to me and my home. I use an abalone shell with a bird feather, as this combines all 4 natural elements:

Water: The abalone shell.

Air: The feather guiding smoke towards the heavens.

Fire: The flame and smoke.

Earth: The sacred herb you are burning.

Sage has countless metaphysical benefits and comes in many different blends. It removes negative energy from your surrounds, pets, mind, body and spirit, and anywhere else you cleanse with the smoke.

One of the top questions I get asked is, "How do I keep the smoke smouldering?" This may take practise, but a simple word of advice is, ensure you use your lighter or match to set the sage on fire to generate the heat and flame before beginning to smudge your surrounds.

Top tip: discount stores will often sell "sage"; however, it is best to avoid buying from these types of businesses as, more often than not, the sage is not ethically and sustainably sourced from its country of origin.

 Walk in Beauty

How to use your sage

Step 1. Light the top of your sage in its entirety (until a flame ignites) and blow to create more smoke and smouldering. Blow the smoke around your surrounds or towards yourself (scoop it in your palms and allow it to swirl over your face, heart and head) as this process naturally helps to remove illness and stagnant, low-vibrating and evil energy.

Step 2. Walk into each room of your home to purify your surrounds with the smouldering sage. Please ensure your windows and doors are wide open so the air and smoke flows freely.

Step 3. Place your abalone shell in your desired hand with the sage resting in your shell, and use the feather in your other hand to disperse smoke into all corners of your home. Speak with pure intention and keep it simple.

Step 4. Always give thanks to Great Spirit, Creator (whomever you believe in) and the universe for their presence, protection and guidance.

Step 5. Once you have finished cleansing your space, extinguish your sage by putting it in sand or

> the earth. I usually leave mine to smoulder out naturally as I love the lingering smell it shares.

Step 6. Gratitude is everything, so give thanks to Mother Earth when using sacred herbs, and dispose of them back into the earth, garden or pot plants. Whatever grows in the Earth should be returned to her and should not be discarded as waste. But, again, this is my personal preference, and you may do whatever feels right for you.

I know certain people find sage overpowering or have health conditions that may be triggered due to the aromatic smoke filling the air. So, here are alternative suggestions to purify and cleanse your surrounds ...

Palo Santo holy wood

Palo Santo originates from Peru and is harvested from fallen and dead trees. The branches are ethically collected and cut into aromatic smudge sticks. Again, it is incredibly important to do your research to ensure responsible sourcing of any natural herb or wood. Palo is sadly becoming scarcer, so I usually only burn mine once a week as it is not as abundant as it once was.

 Walk in Beauty

This beautifully sacred aromatic wood encourages good fortune, harmony, positive energy and protection, and clears your home and surrounds of negative or evil energies. Just like with sage, keeping your Palo Santo smouldering will require practise.

Be mindful and select a more abundant herb whenever you can as the seasons bring natural change to nature. We can follow this prompt by choosing, for example, lavender, cedar or pine when they are in their peak growth. It also gives you the opportunity to try a new herb and aroma.

How to use your Palo Santo

Step 1. Light one end of the Palo Santo stick for 30 seconds to 1 minute or until a flame ignites.

Step 2. Ensure your Palo Santo stick and flame is tilted in a slightly downwards position as this will help ignite and maintain the flame.

Step 3. Once the Palo Santo stick is smoking, you may begin to cleanse your surrounds, following the sage instructions above.

Incense sticks, cones and resins

Incense, cones and resins have been used for centuries for their health benefits. These highly aromatic creations are made using plant-based, natural ingredients. Common ingredients include seeds, bark, flowers, leaves and petals.

These popular creations are slow burning and do not require ongoing effort on your part to keep them burning like sage or Palo Santo would. Having said this, you still need to set a clear intention before lighting your incense, cones or resin if you wish to use their aromatic fragrance and smoke for clearing purposes.

Many people love to use these sticks for relaxation purposes and to bring ambience to their surrounds. You will find certain incense aromas are beneficial for meditation and spiritual growth, and to promote deeper and peaceful sleep. They are cost effective too!

Our range of incense, resins and cones originate from India, and our suppliers give back to the farming communities who grow and supply the herbs, flowers and plants, which is a wonderful and ethical process.

Walk in Beauty

Singing bowls

Singing bowls are traditionally used by monks, Buddhists, light workers, healers, and of course anyone who loves spirituality and sound clearing. They are beautiful creations that promote harmony, peace and balance within our home, and benefit both our mind and body with their healing sounds.

Singing bowls can be used in crystal cleansing, sound clearing, relaxation and meditation practice. They help in clearing any residual negativity or stress you may be carrying within you after a busy day at work or dealing with negative people.

Most singing bowls are created using auspicious metals or crystal, and their sound is incredibly unique. Some bowls are harder to use than others, depending on the style and type of metal used. The shape and size of the singing bowl rim also contributes to the pitch of the sound and the ease of playing. If you are after a specific note and pitch, you are better choosing a crystal bowl; however, they are expensive and, in all honesty, they all do the same job!

How to use your singing bowl

Step 1. Gently hold the base of the bowl in one open palm. Using the wooden striker with the other hand, rotate around the outer rim of the bowl. It's essential to relax the hand you're holding your singing bowl with, so the bowl is balancing lightly on your palm. If you hold it too tightly, you will restrict the sound and it may feel clunky. Larger bowls may be left on their own cushion as they can be heavy or fragile.

Step 2. Your singing bowl will "sing" in high pitches and deliver a traditional *OM*-like sound that naturally invokes feelings of inner peace and relaxation. You can continue to play your singing bowl using circular motions around the outer rim, or you can simply tap a larger-sized singing bowl as the sound will keep vibrating for a longer duration of time.

Step 3. Cleanse your home by walking through each room playing your singing bowl or placing it in the centre of the room, if it is a large one. Allow the sound vibration to remove negative energy and replace it with uplifting, clear and free-flowing energy.

 Walk in Beauty

Step 4. Alternatively, if you want to cleanse your crystals or jewellery, you can place small items in your bowl and proceed to play (not recommended for crystal ones). However, if your crystal and jewellery collection is expansive and located all over your home (guilty as charged), simply hold the singing bowl near your crystals and jewellery and they will naturally receive the clearing vibration.

Witch bells, space clearing bells and brass bells

These beautiful bells are a favourite of mine, and judging by the amount we sell, you all love them too! They also make lovely décor when not in use and add a touch of bohemian and witchy energy wherever you choose to hang them. Brass bells are often placed near or on altars and in sacred spaces around your home for protection. Choose any size or design as they all work equally well. Instead of brass, you may feel drawn to silver or bronze bells.

The pitch of spiritual bells has the following benefits:

- ☾ Placed at the front door, bells help to banish negative energy from entering your home.
- ☾ Perfect for cleansing crystals and possessions.

- ☾ They may be used to clear unwanted energy vibrations or evil spirits.
- ☾ Their sound can help you conjure higher spiritual entities and energies.
- ☾ Wonderful for implementing in spells and manifesting.

Tingsha cymbals/bells

Tingsha bells (also referred to as cymbals) are handmade using traditional brass with ornate designs etched into the surface and are attached to a leather cord. Cymbals are used for our heart chakra, clarity of mind, and for clearing our home of stagnant residual energies. Just like singing bowls, cymbals promote peace, banish negative energy and relax our mind and body, which is important for our wellbeing.

How to use your Tingsha bells/cymbals

Step 1. Using your index finger and thumb, hold the leather cord in the middle so the cymbals hang evenly and freely on each side.

Step 2. Gently swing one cymbal outwards with your free hand, allowing the cymbals to gently tap each other on their outer edge/rim. This simple motion

 Walk in Beauty

of tapping the bells together produces a high-pitched sound vibration.

Step 3. Ensure you allow the vibration and sound to cease completely before striking again.

The Great Spirit

… the voice of the Great Spirit is heard
in the twittering of birds,
the rippling of mighty waters,
and the sweet breathing of flowers.
If this is Paganism, then at present,
at least I am a Pagan.

Gertrude Simmons Bonnin (Zitkala-Sa), 1876–1938. Lakota.

Chapter 7

Everyday self-care

We often neglect tending to our needs and practising regular self-care, don't we? We put everyone and everything else in front of us and, as a result, we are left running on empty. I preach self-care on my website, social media pages and to my Reiki clients and reiterate the importance of "taking time out daily for yourself". The thing is, I used to get so busy and didn't follow my own advice. The reality is … you crash and burn in the long run, when you could have avoided it.

I am going to share several daily self-care rituals that I love to practise and each supports me in staying grounded, connected to nature and promoting feelings of happiness and contentment. They are inexpensive, time-efficient and easy to do, so perhaps you may like to try them, or they will spark ideas for your own self-care practices.

Crystal facial rollers

These simple beauty tools have multiple uses and are an additional way to incorporate crystal healing into your daily schedule. I use my roller twice daily after cleansing my face morning and night. Crystals rollers help your skin absorb serums more easily, and they also make your face feel amazing too.

Rollers increase our blood flow, which helps improve circulation, and this promotes healthy skin. Why stress over wrinkles? They are an honour we earn throughout our life; they show our many life paths and wisdom gained on this current earthly visit. If only Western culture would embrace growing older as most Indigenous people do! They hold so much love and respect for their elders. Our beautiful elders are here to teach us as they have walked many different paths and have seen so much change in our world.

Rollers are wonderful to use under your eyes, and they are heaven sent for soothing sinus pain, when chilled. In summer or when you're feeling hot, you can place your roller in the fridge for 10 minutes before use and it will help to ease facial puffiness and make you look rejuvenated.

Another way to use rollers is for body pains. I suffer with chronic neck pain and find crystal rollers allow me to massage the delicate areas of my neck that I otherwise couldn't reach. I use gentle but firm pressure and massage the area for a few minutes to help lessen the tension. In fact, you can use your roller on any part of your body if you have tension, aches or pains as they are sturdy little things.

Yoni eggs

Made from different crystals, yoni eggs are egg-shaped stones that you wear inside your vagina. This is one self-care department every goddess needs to dedicate time to. Forget about feelings of embarrassment or taboo topics that are not spoken of! This part of our body is sacred and gave life to all of us, so the least we can do is treat her with the respect she deserves.

The recent generations are open and accepting of subjects relating to yoni health, sexual wellness, peri-menopause, menopause and menstruation, whereas in the older days these subjects were not spoken about publicly. I know some of you may feel uncomfortable about these concepts but try and let that feeling go. It is empowering when you begin connecting to your sacred womb energy.

While the exact history of yoni eggs is unknown, accounts date back centuries in Ancient China where yoni eggs were used for sexual health by women. In today's society, it has become increasingly popular for women of all ages in all cultures to use yoni eggs for sexual wellness and strengthening pelvic floor muscles.

Yoni eggs help to empower our sacred feminine energy and sacral chakra. I have used them in my spiritual health practice for the past several years to prevent potential yoni-related problems later down the track. For me, prevention is better than trying to cure something that may have been avoided with simple daily use.

For all us goddesses out there, yoni eggs are going to change your world in a positive way! They help us address the forever-arising obstacles with our changing body, from ageing and hormonal imbalances to fluctuating oestrogen levels, etc.

Yoni eggs can help you with the following issues:

- Urine leakage
- Mild prolapse
- Vaginal dryness
- Peri-menopause and menopause
- Pregnancy

- After childbirth
- Lack of nerve sensations
- Increasing natural vaginal lubrication (this is a necessity for daily comfort, not to mention your sex life)!

Stop blushing because sex is a healthy and natural part of life. It releases good endorphins, makes your skin glow, releases stress and encourages a good night's sleep. Plus, it also keeps your vaginal muscles in use and strengthened.

How to use yoni eggs

Yoni eggs come in a set of 3, and as you progress to each size you gain strength in your pelvic muscles. You start with the largest egg, followed by the medium egg, and lastly the small egg. You may choose to use yoni eggs with or without a string – it all comes down to personal preference. All of our yoni eggs are drilled for convenience and ease of use.

Yoni eggs are incredibly simple to use. You gently insert one egg into your yoni, in the same way you would a tampon. The egg is then held in place by your pelvic floor muscles. Sometimes the egg may fall out if you don't have any pelvic strength, but don't give up as this is exactly what these eggs are designed to help with! If your egg falls out, take a moment to sit or lie down once you insert your egg because then gravity will not have control.

When the egg is in place, you really will not feel it, but you will know it's there, if that makes sense? Now, with the egg in place, start doing pelvic floor squeezes. The easiest way is to imagine you are going to urinate but then stop yourself. Squeeze those pelvic floor muscles like you mean it! Stop start, stop start, stop start. When you squeeze, hold for around 5 seconds each time and do this for as long as you can.

I have a ritual of squeezing 50 times because I turn 50 this year (I'm laughing as I write this), and for me this number works! I use the smallest egg and choose a different crystal depending on my current energy and needs.

Yoni eggs can be used as often as you desire, but the more regularly you practise the better the results. You may notice that your pelvic muscles become tired or even feel heavy (like when you have your period) when you first start using your yoni eggs. This is completely natural and a positive sign they are working their magick. Like with any exercise, your body has to adapt to the new routine.

I usually keep my egg in for a few hours, do 50 squeezes to start off with for a few minutes, and then leave it in place. This will make you laugh but I usually become so busy that

Walk in Beauty

I forget I put one in and only remember when I need to urinate. I like to keep it real, so here is a word of warning for you: Do not take the risk and urinate with your egg in or it may projectile out into the toilet. Yes, I speak from experience, ha-ha!

The only time you should refrain from using yoni eggs is during your moon time (menstrual cycle), if you have thrush, or if you're experiencing vaginal tenderness. Providing you have a healthy pregnancy with no complications, yoni eggs are perfectly safe to use when pregnant and will help keep your pelvic floor muscles healthy and strong for your baby's delivery.

Cleaning yoni eggs is easy too. After use, just wash them with a soap-free cleanser in cold or lukewarm water, and air or towel-dry them. They love a recharge in the sun or moonlight too. Choose whatever crystal you love to work with or feel drawn to as no crystal energy is better than another. It all comes down to the actual egg itself and the effort you put in that does all the work. I love working with clear quartz, fire agate and rose quartz.

On our website we have yoni eggs in a range of crystal energy including clear quartz, new jade, rose quartz, sodalite, rhodonite, red jasper, amethyst, green aventurine, opalite, fluorite, tiger's eye, and lapis lazuli.

Now that I have piqued you interest (fingers crossed) and you feel the call to try yoni eggs, just a little reminder to ensure you buy natural crystal ones from a reputable business. We ensure all our yoni eggs are genuine crystal, body safe and intended for internal body use. We have used the same trusted business who have been making our yoni eggs for the past several years.

Normal crystal eggs have a different outer surface polish on them compared to yoni eggs, so please do not use them as they may do more harm than good. If you want further information on yoni eggs, please email me your questions anytime; I'm happy to help and break the taboo associated with yoni health.

Four directions ritual

Expressing gratitude for everything we have is something to celebrate daily. When we dedicate time to appreciating the small things in life, this practice naturally boosts our feelings of happiness, contentment and peace.

Every morning upon waking, I stand on our balcony overlooking Mount Cooroy and express my gratitude to the universe for everything I have. This ritual happens before I do anything on my to-do list, regardless of the weather or what time I wake up.

 Walk in Beauty

I walk outside barefoot and salute the "four directions". I use my ritual feather and the selenite wand I made, and I raise my glass of water as a symbol of life, as without water we cannot survive or flourish. I call upon my ancestors, spirit animals and Mother Nature for the day ahead. I ask my spirit guides for guidance, protection and healing, and to teach me anything I may need to learn in my journey.

I then say a few words to each direction and send gratitude and love to Great Spirit/Creator and my deceased loved ones. Below, I will share with you how I perform this ritual; however, I will not share the words I use to connect with my spirit guides as this is my sacred communication and is shared with the higher spiritual realms only.

There is no right or wrong way for you to honour and pay gratitude to the four directions, and you may also choose to honour Father Sun (above), Mother Earth (below), and Spirit (within). I hope this routine brings you inner peace because it brings me great happiness, and I could not imagine skipping this beautiful daily ritual.

How to do the four directions ritual

Step 1. Choose your sacred object (mine is a glass of filtered water and my selenite feather wand).

Step 2. With your object, give an offering to the earth around you as a way of expressing gratitude. With my full glass of water I give an offering to the earth below me or a plant nearby. I pour some water out as a way of expressing gratitude and drink the remainder, and then commence facing the four directions.

Step 3. I salute the east. I thank Father Sun for rising and bringing life to us. Every day is a new beginning and the sun shares positivity and new paths ahead.

Step 4. I salute the south. I thank the cold winds that blow change upon us from this direction during autumn and winter. The wind reminds us to continually transform ourselves rather than remaining the same. We are guided to release what no longer serves us as the wind blows around and through us.

Step 5. I salute the north. I thank the spring and summer warmth and the brightest part of Father Sky. The sky shares life-force energy, growth and endurance with us.

Step 6. I salute the west. I thank this direction for the ending of each day, and I look forward to seeing

the stars and Grandmother Moon. The west brings the most thunderstorms and turbulence, and the Thunderbird resides in this direction. He is symbolic of power, protection and strength, and for me this is my favourite direction.

*I hope you enjoy this sacred ritual,
and may it brighten your day as it does mine. A'ho.*

Bath time with crystals

I adore baths, and if I had the time to bathe every night, I absolutely would! I normally spend an hour in the bath reading a book, so you can see why I only have limited time to enjoy this luxury. This isn't necessarily a bad thing because then I really look forward to my "me time" every Friday night and weekends.

Don't get me wrong, a hot shower is relaxing, renewing and beautiful too, and I realise not everyone has a bath in their home or necessarily enjoys having one. This is why I've included a list of salts and crystals that can be used in both baths *and* showers or placed in a bowl for soaking your feet and hands (like having a manicure/pedicure at home).

Bath rituals are a simple self-care practice for me, but it is safe to say my bath doesn't usually resemble the pretty photos on social media, which feature coloured petals from an assortment of flowers, exotic coloured water, and a million candles surrounding the bath edges.

I simply use mineral salts, milks and essentials oils, water-safe crystals, and then light a candle and read an enjoyable book. It makes the clean-up afterward a whole lot easier too. I used to love rose petals and bath bombs but the clean-up after was far from a relaxing experience!

I love using the following crystals and, yes, they may be submerged in water for a brief period of time without damage. Or you may choose to leave them on your shower shelf or on a bath tray above your water (I do both).

Rose quartz

Key phrase: Love and forgiveness.

Purpose: A crystal with mother caring energy, making her the perfect talisman to use during pregnancy by holding her on your stomach to connect with your unborn baby. Rose quartz is a nurturing stone that offers unconditional love and healing for depression, post-natal depression, and helps you overcome abuse of any kind.

 Walk in Beauty

Rose quartz helps us to forgive and respect and encourages reconciliation with ourselves and others. She is metaphysically healing for hormones, fertility, headaches, balance issues and promoting the flow of fluids within our body. If you struggle with nightmares, rose quartz will help banish negative energy and promote sweet dreams and peaceful sleep.

Apophyllite

Key phrase: Spirituality and peace.

Purpose: Apophyllite is Reiki in a crystal form! She is a powerful stone that can stimulate your psychic abilities and help you develop a deeper connection with your spirit guides and angels. Apophyllite promotes peace, harmony and calming energies wherever you choose to place her in your home.

If you need to heal emotions or relationships, apophyllite helps to bring people together and clear the air of stagnant energy and emotional residue. She is metaphysically healing for asthma, hay fever and respiratory problems.

Emerald green calcite

Key phrase: Healing and vitality.

Purpose: A stone sacred to all Earth spirits and Earth healers from Native North America and Scandinavia. Emerald green calcite helps remove negative and stagnant energy from your surrounds and increases vitality within the household.

Emerald green calcite is a highly active and energising crystal that encourages spiritual growth, removes stress, and instils harmony, positivity and peace. She is metaphysically healing for colds and flus, infections and lymph glands.

Shiva lingam

Key phrase: Fertility and libido.

Purpose: These beautiful river rocks are collected after the monsoon season once a year in India. They are gathered from the holy waters of the Narmada River. Shiva lingams are wonderful for inducing harmonious balance within our yin–yang energy. They bring strength and love to your relationships, are symbolic of fertility, and can be used in tantric practices.

 Walk in Beauty

Place a shiva lingam in your bedroom when trying to conceive, and then charge each month under the moon and lunar rays to keep the calming energy flowing through your surrounds. Metaphysically, shiva lingams are healing for fertility, impotence and other sexual dysfunctions, and for increasing libido. You can also use this stone as an all-over body massager to target pressure points, and you can place them in your bath as they have a strong affinity with water too.

Earthing/grounding with Mama Earth

Dedicating time to ground yourself is essential. Mother Earth offers healing medicine to us as she shares negative ions that we absorb through the soles of our feet, and, yes, science has proven this to be true! The natural negative ion energy helps lower blood pressure, boosts the immune system and improves mental health/mindset.

You can ground yourself anywhere, anytime, so long as you have access to the outdoors or even looking out of a window at natural scenery. The sky, birds, trees and flowers can decrease stress levels and bring you back to the present moment. So, where will you go to ground yourself next? Perhaps a beach, a forest, your backyard, your balcony, a local park or a river ... Anywhere in nature is beneficial for our wellbeing!

Get out in nature, dedicate time to regularly grounding yourself, and don't let excuses get in the way. Once you begin, you will be so glad you started this simple yet effective daily practice.

Living with health issues

Not all of us breeze through life without a few curveballs along the way. I have suffered with chronic nerve pain called cervical radiculopathy for 18 years now, and it is a harsh ailment to have. I rely on prescribed 24-hour dosages of slow-release medication to ease my pain and keep me mobile so I can do what I love, as surgery is not an option for me.

In 2022, I was diagnosed with Hashimoto's disease, which is an autoimmune disorder that attacks the thyroid. I now take daily medication for the rest of my life to control my hormone production and body inflammation. Hashimoto's, like all autoimmune diseases, has its flare-ups, and I have good and bad days, so I take them as they come.

For me, the saddest part of my diagnosis is the hair loss I have suffered. I have lost nearly half of my hair and it has left

 Walk in Beauty

me in tears and feeling really down. One sleepless night (I would lie awake thinking about my hair loss), I considered getting hair extensions. I'm happy to say, since deciding to get them, they have profoundly changed my life while I try to grow back years' worth of hair.

At the time of writing this book, I am feeling super-confident because I have gorgeous long locks that blend into my natural hair and make me feel like a goddess. I named my hair extensions "Cynthia" (I realise some of you may think this is strange, but I needed to name them), and I am incredibly grateful to the woman who cut her hair for those of us in need. I thank my daughter Taylar for doing my extensions every month. So much gratitude!

There is usually something we can do to boost our spirit and help our self-esteem and confidence. Never give up on doing simple rituals that make you feel better about yourself, and always surround yourself with a beautiful support team.

Something I am so grateful for is my supportive family and best friend, whom I met when our children were in preschool. I refer to Colleen as my "sis" because she's the sister I never had! She also has her share of health issues but has helped me immensely over the last year after my diagnosis of Hashimoto's.

Chapter 7

I share my health issues not for sympathy but to shine a light for other people who may be dealing with chronic health problems also. Within reason, you can still do many of the things you love, if you are willing to try and adapt to new ways of doing things. Age is also not a barrier – I am doing more things now in my life then I ever thought possible, and I didn't accomplish any of these goals when I was younger and healthier.

Crystals and spirituality play a huge role in my life and have helped me to understand that life doesn't have to be perfect all the time. Crystals support my wellbeing and make me feel blissful. My love for Mother Earth and all her crystal creations is never-ending, and I just cannot imagine life without them.

I know many people judge and imply that "true spiritual people" don't take prescribed medication, they only consume vegan food and use organic products, avoid dairy, and do juice cleanses and intermittent fasting, only take natural supplements ... essentially, they do everything we don't do!

But who cares what other people do? We each have our own journey, and it's important to stay on your own path and do what works best for your body and health. I eat everything in moderation and follow no specific diet

Walk in Beauty

because I have no intolerances at this point in my life. My daily bliss is savouring 3 cups of coffee with full-cream milk, and the simple task of brewing my latte makes my heart sing!

For a Reiki Master, I break most of the rules "they say" regarding not eating before healings, avoiding caffeine, taking medications, etc., but do you know what? What I do works great for me and my clients. I have been doing Reiki for over 4 years now, and I have never had a complaint. I love what I do, I have a deep passion for it, and I have my own approach, as most healers do.

So, just as I have found what works best for me, you can do the same. My advice is simple: ignore what other people do and/or what social media glorifies as the "right way" to live your life. Instead, focus on creating self-care rituals, routines and practices that work best for your energy level, health circumstances, age, and your mental and physical capabilities.

Daily rituals don't need to cost a fortune, nor do they need to be time-consuming if you can only devote a few minutes to them in your busy daily schedule. Simply do whatever makes you feel happy!

If you love writing, you could start journalling about the experiences that have shaped you into the person you are today, the lessons you have learned along the way, and the skills you've developed over the years. You do not have to journal solely about positive experiences – that would be impossible due to the ups and downs we all experience in life.

If you love reading, why not dedicate time before bed to getting lost in an enjoyable book that helps switch your mindset to somewhere other than where you are right now? Books are invaluable; they teach us, they encourage us, they inspire us and sometimes we never want a good book to end.

If you love nature, why not watch the sunrise if you are a morning person (nope not me)? My Goddess Mama is a "get up and at 'em" person and has a lot of energy. She runs rings around me in that department, and she also takes no prescription medicines in her mid-70s. We call her "Morning Sun" as it describes her perfectly – a ray of sunshine and energy! So, when you next feel the warmth of a new day, perhaps say a few positive words to start the day off on the right foot. Every new day is your opportunity to try something new and be thankful for your life.

If you aren't a morning person, why not watch the sunset? I watch the sunset every evening and find it incredibly relaxing. If you love the energy of the approaching night

 Walk in Beauty

and are a night owl, embrace that feeling and go and sit in the cool air under the dark skies. Have a conversation with the universe and release any worries from your day.

Take a deep breath, relax your jaw, drop your shoulders and let your body feel limp. Everything usually feels better after a good night's sleep, especially your overall wellbeing and health. Our body relaxes, rejuvenates and repairs as much as it can as we rest, so ensure you are getting enough peaceful sleep to heal your body.

Lastly, leave any toxic energy outside your home and aura! Sage yourself more regularly, manifest abundance towards yourself, and leave no room for negative thinking as it will not benefit you or your health ailments.

Try to spend less time worrying about work, finances, health and relationships because you can only do so much. Your energy is valuable and it directly affects your health, so always treat it and yourself with the highest of respect because you deserve it.

Mother Earth to the Spirit World

What is life?
It is the flash of a firefly in the night.
It is the breath of a buffalo in the winter time.
It is the little shadow which runs across the grass
And then loses itself in the Sunset.

**Crowfoot, as he prepared for his journey
to the spirit world, 1890. Blackfoot.**

Chapter 8

Working with the moon phases

I always follow the lunar cycles and moon phases. Working with lunar energy has changed my life, enhanced my spiritual growth and improved my mental focus. Many years before I embarked on my spiritual journey, I can honestly say that I closed every door and blind in our home on the full moon because I was strongly affected by the lunar energy and would suffer with insomnia for days leading up to it.

My beautiful aunty was the same, and we would often send messages to each other around the full moon and laugh about it! Fast forward to the present day, and thank goodness my eyes were opened to how much magick the lunar phases have to offer us if we choose to embrace them. If we set our intention to become in sync with her lunar phases, we will find our energy will begin to naturally ebb and flow like the ocean tides.

Even our menstrual cycle (moon time) is influenced by the moon and her mysterious energy. The word "menstruation" originates from the Greek and Latin word "mene", which means moon. Countless cultures believe women to be most intuitive during their sacred "moon time" cycle.

In Native American tradition, when women were menstruating they gathered in a separate moon lodge from their normal dwelling, and their chores were completed by other family members. During their moon time it was believed that women could make deeper spiritual connections within dreams of meditative quests and connect with Great Spirit/Creator because their spiritual power was at its strongest peak.

Imagine how wonderful it would be if we had this privilege in today's society? How beautiful it would be! There are many easy rituals we can practise during the moon phases and, of course, at any time during the month. So, let us explore these below.

New moon

A time for new beginnings. New moon is wonderful for manifesting and planting seeds of intention for the weeks and months ahead. Think of your thoughts like a garden;

 Walk in Beauty

you need to keep nurturing these intentions so that they flourish. If you manifest something into the universe and then forget about it, how will it happen?

You need to take the initiative, invest personal effort and work hard on your dreams because manifesting alone will not lead to things falling into your lap. Additionally, you should regularly check in with yourself and reflect on the effort you are investing into your dream because this is when manifestation becomes powerful and full of magick! Using crystals when you manifest and during the new moon is a powerful way to raise the energy vibration.

You may like to start a journal or create a vision board of photos and your favourite mantras that relate to your aspirations and goals. I wish upon a star as I find that works best for me. I love talking to the night sky and find it incredibly relaxing.

Drawing an oracle card from your favourite deck during this moon phase is a wonderful way to become inspired and reinforce the magick you are hoping to achieve. When I work with oracle cards, I ask a simple question, shuffle the cards until it feels intuitively right to stop, and then reveal my chosen card. To further amplify the spiritual guidance of my oracle card, I place it on my bookshelf, surround it with empowering crystals and leave it on display for a week.

As we established earlier, we all resonate with crystal shapes and their metaphysical energies differently. I love using crystals based on their ability to connect with the moon phases.

The new moon often brings energising and uplifting energy to our spiritual bodies, and we can further enhance our connection to the lunar cycle by using the following crystals.

Rainbow moonstone

Key phrase: Intuition and lunar energy.

Purpose: Moonstone encompasses all things celestial and lunar related. Moonstone is a wonderful talisman for new beginnings, attracting abundance, opening ourselves up to new pathways, and for connecting with our spirituality and psychic gifts.

This crystal has a strong connection to feminine energy and is perfect to use for enhancing your intuition and psychic abilities during the new moon phase. Moonstone empowers our crown, third eye and sacral chakras – the trio of creativity and inspiration to follow our dreams.

 Walk in Beauty

Labradorite

Key phrase: Psychic abilities and magick.

Purpose: Labradorite is associated with mystical energy and magick with all her flashes of blue, purple, green and gold! She is like the aurora borealis. Labradorite reminds us to enjoy the present moment and break free of the daily grind whenever we have the chance. Embrace a little spontaneity and see if you enjoy it.

Labradorite is a spiritual stone for developing our third eye, delving into psychic work and during meditative practice. She helps our chakras become aligned, offers protection and encourages self-confidence.

Carnelian

Key phrase: Vitality and fertility.

Purpose: Carnelian is a vibrant life-force energy that attracts fertility (in all areas) of our life. She ignites our inner flame and creativity and connects us with Goddess Isis and all her healing energy.

Carnelian is reminiscent of the setting sun, and connecting with her energy allows us to discover joy, happiness and increased motivation. She is healing for sexual problems, boosts fertility and libido, and if you need help during your menstrual cycle, carry a carnelian tumble stone in your bra or pocket.

Moss agate

Key phrase: Grounding and nurturing.

Purpose: Moss agate is beautiful for encouraging new growth, embarking on new paths and nurturing yourself. Agate is an ancient healer that brings yin–yang balance into our wellbeing and surroundings, which is important for a healthy, productive and harmonious life.

Agate increases our stamina to ensure we finish all the tasks we have started and provides a sense of inner security and peace of mind. Placing a piece of agate in plants or resting on your journal will remind you to always keep growing and flourishing where you are, to not worry about the uncertainties of the future, and to enjoy your life right now.

Agate is healing for our overall health, encouraging deep sleep and easing nightmares, and helps us feel grounded and connected to Mother Earth.

Clear quartz

Key phrase: White-light energy and empowerment.

Purpose: Clear quartz naturally intensifies the energy of any crystal we use, not to mention it surrounds us with white-light energy and healing from our root to crown chakra. Quartz is incredibly easy to program and is a must-have crystal in everyone's collection. Manifesting with clear quartz empowers your thoughts and mindset, and you can use it anywhere, anytime.

Quartz is a highly protective crystal and is ideal to work with if you feel someone has directed ill-wishing or evil energy your way. Surround yourself in a bubble of white light by using a clear quartz wand or natural point and guiding it in a clockwise direction around your physical body.

Full moon

The full moon phase possesses a stronger lunar energy than the new moon. It can often enhance our emotional reactions and leave us feeling exhausted and drained. Since early civilisation, the power that emanates from the full moon phase has been recognised as spiritual and symbolic of endings. Some people feel empowered during the full moon, yet others the complete opposite. Your zodiac sign and the season Grandmother Full Moon takes place in can influence how you react to her energy.

The full moon encourages us to shed any emotional, mental or spiritual layers and release any negativity that may be halting our progress in life. Remember, you hold the power within your higher self, so when you combine it with the full moon lunar energy, you can move mountains if you set your mind to it. Never give up!

I always change up my crystals depending on my needs, but here is a list of crystals that work well with the heightened full moon lunar phase:

Black obsidian

Key phrase: Magick and protection.

Purpose: Black obsidian is a beautiful glossy black colour and supports us in releasing past trauma, negative thought patterns and self-beliefs, and prompts us to develop a positive outlook on life and ourselves. Obsidian is protective and offers grounding earth vibrations that coincide with our root chakra.

Black obsidian is often used in spells and rituals because of the healing properties of the naturally reflective silica volcanic glass. If you're looking for a crystal that offers

 Walk in Beauty

grounding, stability and protective energy during the heightened full moon phase, then black obsidian is for you.

Tiger's eye

Key phrase: Abundance and empowerment.

Purpose: Tiger's eye is an amazing crystal of chatoyant colours that vary depending on the shades of light and angles you hold it. The colours may change from deep earthy browns to golden yellow, which will shimmer every time you move the crystal. Tiger's eye gifts us with inner strength and confidence, boosts our vitality, and activates our solar plexus.

This crystal is wonderful for increasing abundance and wealth if you have a business or are pursuing a new career venture. Tiger's eye offers support if you suffer with digestive issues or lethargy by holding the power of both Father Sun and Mother Earth within her.

Selenite

Key phrase: Spirituality and lunar energy.

Purpose: I could not bypass this beautiful stone. Selenite is named after the Moon Goddess Selene, so it goes without saying she is a wonderful energy to work with during any lunar phase. Selenite is a harmonious, high-vibrating crystal, perfect for meditation and psychic development.

You can place selenite on your windowsill to keep bad spirits and energy away from your home, and direct moonlight will always keep her fully charged.

Green aventurine

Key phrase: Transformation and luck.

Purpose: We all need a little good luck now and again! Green aventurine is a nature crystal that offers gentle healing and is amplified when used outside while connecting to Mother Earth. Her energy becomes more powerful every time you touch her, so ensure you regularly work with her whenever you are outdoors, wanting to connect with the nature spirits, or simply when you need crystal healing.

Green aventurine helps clear feelings of sadness and emotional upheaval, and offers support through life changes. A beautiful crystal that offers support with anxiety and fertility, and acts as a good-luck talisman for attracting blessings.

 Walk in Beauty

Waning moon phase

The waning moon occurs after the full moon and before the new moon. This lunar phase guides us to relax and engage in self-reflection as the moon energy becomes less intense and gentler with her healing. As the moon becomes smaller in size, this is our indicator to withdraw and distance ourselves from the things that cause us stress. Use the waning moon to sit in stillness, renew your energy, spend more time in nature and dedicate time to spoiling yourself.

The following crystals work wonderfully with the waning moon.

Lepidolite

Key phrase: Higher self and transformation.

Purpose: Lepidolite is beautiful for bringing balance and positive changes in your life. She amplifies our connection with the cosmos and increases our relationship and awareness of our higher self and authentic self.

Lepidolite has soft, nurturing energy that is perfect for meditating with and resolving longstanding issues and patterns of behaviour that are holding you back from moving forward in your life journey.

Blue aragonite

Key phrase: Spiritual ascension and healing.

Purpose: A wonderful crystal that provides clear thinking, common sense and stability within your life. If you are embarking on a new business or creative venture, or learning new skills in your profession or personal life, blue aragonite will ease any feelings of stress, anxiety and overwhelm associated with change.

Aragonite helps you ascend to the higher spiritual realms where angels and spirit guides reside. By holding a piece in your palms while grounding in nature, you will amplify the natural healing and grounding energy aragonite has to offer. If you have any lingering anger from the past, aragonite will support you in releasing this blocked energy and encourage self-growth.

Petrified wood

Key phrase: Dreams and healing.

Purpose: Petrified wood is found in Australia and is a stone of transformation and spirituality, so is often used in healing work. It has an incredibly grounding and earth-based energy, which protects us from evil and negativity.

 Walk in Beauty

If you delve into dreams, astral projection, or practise meditation before bedtime, petrified wood helps you connect with departed loved ones and spirit guides in the higher realms. If you suffer with back pain, allergies or hay fever, petrified wood may help ease your symptoms.

Waxing moon phase

The waxing moon phase occurs between a half moon leading up to a full moon. This lunar phase guides us to open ourselves up to new ideas, actions and pathways. If you have a dream or goal in mind, the waxing moon phase is the time to start planning and moving forwards with the next steps.

Spend a little more time being active, push yourself through any obstacles, and embark on the path that is meant for you. By laying the groundwork now, you set the course of action for yourself over the coming weeks and months.

The following crystals work wonderfully with the waxing moon.

Amazonite

Key phrase: Love and luck.

Purpose: Amazonite is a stone of courage, luck and calming energies. Carry her with you as a lucky talisman when entering competitions or if a burst of luck is needed. Amazonite removes negative energy, irritability, anger and energy blocks in the body.

She increases feelings of self-respect and supports us in manifesting universal love and peace. Amazonite provides protection against electromagnetic pollution, deflects negativity and offers healing for sore throats, thyroid conditions and recovery after illness.

Apatite

Key phrase: Karma and willpower.

Purpose: Apatite is also referred to as "Bones of the Earth". She cleanses our aura and connects with all our chakras to promote balance and harmony. Apatite is a powerful dream stone to activate your intuition and to help you recall past lives or karmic patterns so you can recognise what you need to change or be mindful of in your current life.

 Walk in Beauty

Apatite will increase the healing properties of natural therapies and enhance the vibration of other crystals when used alongside her. She is wonderful if you want to increase your motivation and willpower to pursue life goals. If you have brittle bones, fluid imbalances or your metabolism needs a kick-start, amazonite is perfect for you.

Bumble bee jasper

Key phrase: Faith and vitality.

Purpose: A gorgeous stone with vibrant patterns that originates from Australia. Bumble bee jasper encourages us to be honest with ourselves and provides us with strength to overcome obstacles. She infuses us with boosted vitality and, just like the humble bumble bee, provides us with a natural buzz!

Bumble bee inspires us to have the courage to take a leap of faith, say yes to new ideas, and boosts our initiative and self-confidence. If you suffer with addiction, gaze into the patterns of this lovely stone as it will serve as a distraction to naturally help you shift your mindset and focus. Bumble bee is metaphysically healing for stress, lethargy, IBS, easing stomach dis-ease due to stress, and is boosting for your immune system.

Moon water

Moon water is water infused with moonlight rays. You can place filtered water in any sized jug, mug or vase, and if you intend to place it outdoors under the moonlight, please always use a lid. If you prefer to leave your jug of water indoors, simply place it in a position during the night where it will receive moonlight (a windowsill is perfect) for a few hours as this is all it needs to charge your water.

You can place your chosen crystals on top or beside your jug to further amplify and charge your moon water with crystal and lunar vibrations. Your crystals do not need direct contact with the water, and, in fact, I advise against doing this. You receive the same healing benefits by placing your crystals beside your water without any potential toxic side-effects or nasties getting ingested.

Next, you may choose to write down your intentions and prayers or say them aloud while you hold your palms over your jug of water and crystals. Keep your words simple and straight to the point. Once you have spoken aloud or written down your words, thank your spirit guides and walk away from your water because your intention has been sent out into the universe to be heard by the higher spiritual realms.

 Walk in Beauty

When you awaken the next morning, enjoy a glass of your moonlight-infused water. I love using it in my coffee, tea and for my pot plants, and you can use it for your pets' water bowls too!

Hair cutting and growth

Hair is incredibly sacred to me, and this stems from my Cherokee blood. I experience anxiety and panic at the thought of trimming my hair, and although some people may find this silly, it's actually not! Hair is considered sacred in many cultures around the world, and every religious, spiritual and cultural belief system associates different symbology to hair.

Many Native American tribes believe their hair ties them to Mother Earth and is symbolic of long pieces of grass. This is what the sacred herb sweetgrass represents; it is a braid of 3 sections. Long braided hair to Native Americans symbolises being united with our Creator as hair is an extension of our soul.

Have you ever thought of tending to your locks in alignment with the moon phases?

It is believed that the various moon phases and lunar energy can encourage hair growth and slow it down (perfect if you have bangs). Being a moonchild (Cancerian) that is ruled by lunar energy, I try to follow the moon phases if I can as I have naturally slower-growing hair. To accelerate hair growth, schedule your haircut during the waxing phase of the moon (leading up to the full moon).

To slow your hair growth, you need to reverse the lunar phases and organise your haircut during the waning phase of the moon (wind down after the full moon and the lead up to the new moon phase). Also invest in a luxurious hair masque too because treatments can be done at any time.

 Walk in Beauty

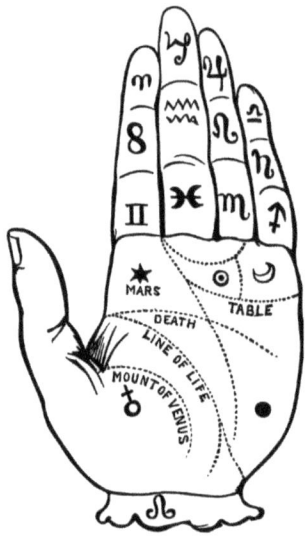

The Great Spirit

The Great Spirit is all things;
he is in the air we breathe.
The Great Spirit is our Father,
but the Earth is our Mother.
She nourishes us;
that which we put into the ground returns to us...

Big Thunder (Bedagi), late 19th century. Wabanaki Algonquin.

Chapter 9

Reiki energy healing

Have you ever wondered what Reiki is and how to pronounce it? Allow me to share my understanding of this beautiful, ancient practice and the many benefits it has to offer us ...

"Ray key" is the correct pronunciation.

"Rei" means universal higher power and *"Ki"* means life-force energy. This beautiful, universal energy extends beyond our physical body and reaches our aura and chakras to promote all-over healing.

I have always gravitated towards Reiki. The concept of healing physical and metaphysical dis-ease using universal energy is a wonderful practice. Upon learning this ancient healing modality, my life has changed, and my spiritual gifts have further developed.

There are various levels and teachings attained in Reiki as you progress through each attunement to reach a Master

Walk in Beauty

level. Attunements are a higher vibratory energy that are passed directly from the master to the student. Each learning level allows you to grow and empower yourself while shifting your mind, body and spirit for the greater good. To encompass such energy makes me so grateful!

Usui Reiki was founded by a Japanese-born Buddhist monk named Dr Mikato Usui over 100 years ago. Born in 1865 and passing away in 1926, Dr Usui never wrote down all his Reiki knowledge, yet he shared his teachings and traditions with those seeking to learn the ancient ways of universal healing.

Although we may never learn in great depth the spiritual practices and knowledge from Dr Usui, I feel, as many other Reiki Masters do, that the "not knowing" heightens the spiritual and mysterious energy surrounding this sacred healing practice. Today, Reiki remains one of the most widely used practices in Western energy healing, and numerous variations and symbols of Reiki have since been introduced.

Dr Usui introduced the 5 Reiki Principles, which serve as a daily reminder and have a positive impact on my mindfulness and outlook on life. There are slight variations in the phrases used, depending on the teacher, course or book you are working with, so choose what most resonates with you.

> Reiki Principle 1: *Just for today I will not be angry.*
>
> Reiki Principle 2: *Just for today I will not worry.*
>
> Reiki Principle 3: *Just for today I will do my work honestly.*
>
> Reiki Principle 4: *Just for today I will be grateful for all my blessings.*
>
> Reiki Principle 5: *Just for today I will be kind to all living things.*

These mindful-based principles can help us in our daily life as they encourage us to remain positive, be humble and appreciate the blessings surrounding us. Below, I have included a summary of what the principles mean to me and how you can integrate them into your life.

Just for today I will not be angry

Anger: A fiery emotion that we all experience in our lifetime. There is nothing wrong with experiencing bouts of anger; we are human beings who encounter stress, personalities we clash with, situations that are unfair and beyond our control … Anger is a powerful emotion that should never be deemed negative or something we should suppress and ignore when it arises.

 Walk in Beauty

Principle meaning: A reminder to feel the emotion of anger, honour it, reflect and understand why we are feeling this way, and then let it go. Notice how your anger impacts you. Does it affect a certain chakra? Is there a certain trigger? Does it occur often? How do you manage it? Etc. The intention is to raise your awareness of how you experience anger and how you can heal yourself from holding on to any heaviness, frustration or lingering emotions once the anger has passed.

Anger is often a sign we need to ground ourselves and balance our energy once again. By returning to nature and listening to the trees, feeling the wind against our skin, inhaling the aroma of plants and flowers, and clearing our mind, we will find our anger naturally dissipates.

Just for today I will not worry

Worry: To a certain extent we all worry about things sometimes. This can lead to anxiety, ruminating thoughts and unnecessary stress. I used to be terrible with how much I worried about things. However, since embarking on my spiritual path, I now understand that everything flows as it needs to and to worry is a waste of energy.

Principle meaning: A reminder to check-in with your thoughts and emotions to notice what worries and anxieties are flowing through your mind. Notice what you are worrying about, when the worry arises, how long the worry lasts, etc. The intention is to try to put a positive spin on any situation that arises and be thankful for everything you have in this moment, rather than what you feel is missing in your life.

Worry can be a signal from our higher self that we need to quieten our mind and take a step back from the busyness of our life in an attempt to dedicate more time for relaxation, mindfulness and meditation.

Just for today I will do my work honestly

Honesty: To be authentic means speaking your truth always, walking your walk and honouring your beliefs and morals. Sometimes being honest and authentic can get you into deep water with others, but so be it.

Principle meaning: It is important to stand up for what you believe and embrace your unique self because who wants to be the same as everyone else? It doesn't matter if you're different – it reflects that you don't follow trends or try to mould yourself into something you are not.

The intention is to be mindful of how you are expressing yourself to the world and others, and whether your actions

 Walk in Beauty

and words align with your true self, or whether you have lost parts of yourself trying to appease others.

Just for today I will be grateful for all my blessings

Gratitude: Approaching life with an open mind and humble heart is a beautiful way to experience the world and all it has to offer. No matter how successful, famous, rich or accomplished we become, we must never forget who we are beyond the material and external surface.

Principle meaning: A gentle reminder that blessings appear in various forms, shapes and sizes, and we should be grateful for everything we have. My daily coffee ritual is one of my favourite blessings and brings me bliss with every sip.

Everyday tasks and practices are often overlooked and considered boring because we may be focusing too much on the bigger picture, the long-term goal we are striving to achieve, or manifesting what we want to happen in the future. When we focus too much on what we don't have, we lose our ability to recognise and enjoy everything we have achieved and are blessed with in the here and now.

Chapter 9

Just for today I will be kind to all living things

Kindness: We can strive to be anything in our lifetime but being kind to others is one of the most soulfully rewarding experiences. Helping others does not have to be a challenging task, in fact, it's one of the easiest things we can do.

Offering a smile, compliment or brief chat with a passing stranger can completely turn someone's day around. Think about it like this: you may be the only person who has demonstrated kindness to that person in their day, their week, or, for some, it may be one of the few acts of kindness they have ever received.

Principle meaning: Share positive, loving, non-judgemental, supportive and kind energy whenever you can. Not only are you doing a good deed and supporting others, but you're also encouraging love, healing and new growth to flow through your heart chakra. Certain people may need a sprinkle of your kindness more than you know.

 Walk in Beauty

How Reiki works

Usui Reiki is the practice of transferring life-force healing energy. This is channelled through the Reiki Master's palms and directed to their client. While we cannot see the energy being transferred, we can feel it. Reiki awakens and encourages our body to use its natural healing ability to treat any dis-ease, energy blocks and wellbeing ailments.

During Reiki healing, any dormant, stagnant or negative energy is shifted from the body to allow the life-force energy to flow to exactly where it is needed most. This is the incredible power that universal energy healing has to offer. Practising and receiving Reiki is like receiving a beautiful healing hug, unconditional love and alignment from the cosmos.

Reiki Masters use a series of sacred symbols and hand placements, which are directed to your body (wellbeing), and this process allows you to receive higher energy that is transferred to your mind, body, spirit and emotions.

Reiki energy healing works effectively whether it's via distance or hands-on, and the choice comes down to the client and Reiki Masters' personal preferences. For Reiki healings conducted via long distance, the Hon Sha Ze Sho Nen (distance symbol) is used as it represents "timelessness" and reminds us that no matter where we reside, we can always receive healing and love from the universe. The distance symbol promotes openness and emotional acceptance for us to receive the energy being offered by the Reiki Master.

I offer distant Reiki healings by using a photo and name of the client, which I meditate with prior to beginning the healing session to connect with their energy. Over the years, I have found most clients prefer to be in their own surrounds rather than travelling somewhere to receive a hands-on healing.

It is completely normal at first to feel nervous about accepting energy you have never felt before, and this is why it's important to share your thoughts and concerns with your Reiki Master prior to your healing. I have found being in your own home helps to lessen any nerves you may experience and allows you to relax more deeply. Being relaxed and open during your session often results in a more successful healing as your mind, body and spirit have completely opened and allowed the healing energy to flow through without hesitation.

Everyone responds differently to Reiki; it is quite fascinating actually! Certain people may experience tingling, heat, coolness, goosebumps, sudden bursts in energy, sleepiness or even as though they are floating. However, other people

may feel nothing during the time of their healing (this happens to me and Taylar), yet in the days following, the effects of the healing begin to surface.

Just like crystals, Reiki can trigger unexpected emotions, feelings and sensations to surface within you. Emotional responses are a common reaction after healings, especially if you've experienced past trauma, heartbreak or have been repressing feelings and thoughts. Some people may feel anger, which they need to let go of, and others may feel like they are on cloud nine.

For those of us with chronic pain (raises hand), we may feel an increase or sudden spike in our health ailment or injury; however, this is a normal bodily response and doesn't last long. In fact, it's a wonderful sign from your body that it has received and responded to the Reiki energy being sent.

You may refer to these reactions and responses as a "spiritual detox". They are not harmful in any way and reflect that your body is shifting unwanted energy and emotions, and your chakras are aligning in a harmonious way once again. Remember, though, always continue taking your prescription medication because holistic and modern medicine go hand in hand for a positive outcome.

I always remind people that the effects or symptoms we experience after Reiki are symbolic of the toxic energy that has been dormant in our bodies and is now being cleansed and cleared. Stagnant and blocked energy causes dis-ease within our wellbeing, so it is only natural to feel a little discombobulated, emotional, tired or even energised as this energy is shifted from wherever it was hiding in our mind, body, spirit and emotional bodies.

So how many Reiki healings do you need? The amount of sessions you choose to receive is entirely a personal choice. There is no right or wrong number as we are all unique and dealing with our own struggles and respond to energy healing differently. The good news is, you can never have too much positivity and healing energy! However, it is important to note that Reiki is not a miracle cure, and one stand-alone session won't move mountains.

I find a few Reiki sessions over the course of 1–2 months can work wonders for most clients and their wellbeing. Interestingly, I've noticed that a lot of spiritual people, including light workers, healers and psychics, often have chronic health ailments themselves, and their past experiences, pain and knowledge have guided them to help others find the light at the end of the tunnel and have faith in their healing journey.

Walk in Beauty

If you are still not convinced of the healing benefits of Usui Reiki, here are 11 more ways it can help you:

- ☾ The healing energy will never cause you harm and always has your highest good at heart.
- ☾ Delivers balance and harmony to your body and soul.
- ☾ Delivers peace, stillness and clarity to your mind and thoughts.
- ☾ Removes toxic, blocked or repressed energy from your wellbeing.
- ☾ Reduces your stress levels.
- ☾ Eases pain by relaxing your physical body.
- ☾ Improves sleeping patterns and promotes peaceful sleep.
- ☾ Boosts your immunity.
- ☾ Encourages spiritual growth.
- ☾ Promotes feelings of love and self-compassion.
- ☾ Releases past traumas and heavy emotions.

My intention with this chapter was to open your eyes to the beautiful healing energy of Reiki, and I hope one day you experience a distant or in-person healing session. I offer distant Reiki healing 1:1 sessions weekly through our website; however, I realise not everyone can afford a personal session.

With this in mind, I also use our social media platforms to offer a monthly complimentary group Reiki healing for our followers. I feel like this gesture helps to create a ripple of goodwill, healing, love and positive energy in the world. One of the reasons I embarked on my Reiki journey was to help others in need, and it makes my heart happy to extend the healing energy to everyone who needs it. This includes animals, plants, nature, and anything you want to receive healing.

 Walk in Beauty

Assured

Be it dark; be it bright
Be it pain; be it rest
Be it wrong; be it right
It must be for the best.
Some good must somewhere wait.
And sometime joy and pain
Must cease to alternate
Or else we live in vain.

Poetry of Alex Posey, 19th century. Creek.

Chapter 10

Negative energy and psychic vampires

Over the years, I have learned the valuable lesson of distancing myself in both my private and professional life from "so-called friends" and negative people. It is essential to protect yourself and your surrounds – your home, business, family and possessions – from lower-vibrating people as they can negatively affect your mental, emotional, physical and spiritual wellbeing if you unknowingly allow them into your spiritual bodies (aura and psychic energy).

I am going to share some tips and practices that I use daily to shield myself from negative energy, and additional ways of clearing and cleansing your home and body using spiritual tools that are readily available, cost friendly and effective. You may love the sound of everything I suggest and want to give it all a try, but remember, the objective is to use the clearing approach that provides you with a sense of protection and clarity. I tend to use

a combination of practices and tools depending on the energy I need to clear.

First, let's explore what psychic vampires are.

Psychic vampires

You only need to read folklore legends or ask anyone with a spiritual gift, e.g., a psychic, medium, clairvoyant or healer, to hear how very real psychic vampires are and how deeply they can affect our mindset, health and spiritual energy.

To put it bluntly, psychic vampires suck the life out of you. All your positive energy will naturally deflate after being in their company. Psychic vampires are people attracted to your inner light, love, kindness, empathy, success and life-force energy. They often prey upon your positive and happy energy in a subtle way at first, especially if they start out as a friend to you.

These days, I'm a lot more in-tune with my instincts about people's energy and underlying motives and consider myself intuitively wise after years of developing a deeper sense of trust in the intuitive feelings I receive about others. When I experience the "inner feeling" or "inner knowing" that something doesn't feel right about a person or place, I immediately distance myself and become a ghost to them.

It took me years to rid myself of so-called friends that weren't truly there for me.

The friends in question would ignore my social media posts, never wish me a happy birthday, or support me in growing success. They weren't cheering me on from the sidelines or offering any kind words like friends normally do; however, I didn't initially notice these signs until their negative energy started affecting my dreams and energy.

My family and psychic warned me about these people, but I couldn't see it at the time as I like to see the good in people. But now, I'm happy to say those people are blocked for good reason! They were fake, filled with envy, and spread negativity for no reason other than being unmotivated, envious and lazy.

They would avoid working or doing anything that involved dedicating time, effort and energy and had an excuse for everything. But don't we all have an excuse, such as chronic health, lack of time, feeling tired, too stressed? It's about believing and pushing yourself beyond your comfort zone, so you don't let your excuses or ailments define who you are and what you're capable of doing.

Empower yourself and believe you can do it. Rest as needed and don't let your health define you; it's only part of who

 Walk in Beauty

you truly are. It may, in fact, be a blessing in disguise, just as mine was. It got me here today!

Psychic attack

I'm going to share an experience that shook me to my core. I can still recall the terror I felt in that moment. I'm sure the person who sent this negative energy would love reading this chapter as it would validate her own mind of how dark energy can be projected to others.

I'm sure many of you reading this can relate to encountering or experiencing dark energies, ill-wishing or unwanted spiritual activity. Over the years, I've had several people mention feeling "cursed" or believing that someone has sent negative energy to their health, happiness and loved ones.

My psychic attack experience...

So, I had been friends with a woman on Facebook for many years, even though we had never physically met. We chatted daily about life and personal matters, shared photos and had a lot of laughs. However, the dynamic abruptly changed when I started my business. Her personality altered, she would say things like, "I want your life" and, "You're so lucky!" Then she started criticising my eldest daughter, Taylar, who is successful at what she does – "Tarot Taylar".

Fast forward in time and we eventually had an argument that ended all connections; we blocked each other. I released her toxic and negative energy completely from my life and didn't look back. Until one night …

In a dream, I experienced a visit from the coldest and most evil entity I had ever seen or felt in my life. This being was pure evil, a dark black force with a disfigured face and body with long fingers like rakes. I was in a cold sweat as the entity was scratching her fingers over my entire body.

I couldn't speak and fought back in sheer terror. I shielded my face and surrounded my aura in white-light protective energy. In my mind, I was calling upon my ancestors and spirit guides to further shield me and come to my rescue. The evil entity eventually disappeared into thin air.

I awoke and told Wayne what had happened. I was too shaken to go back to sleep in the early hours of the morning. Without question, I knew intuitively in my mind it was my ex-friend who had conjured and directed this evil energy towards me.

However, what I didn't realise was that she had targeted my entire family with this evil energy. We all had nightmares

the same night and all of them involved harming me and Taylar. Never in my life would I conjure bad energy or direct ill-wishing to someone, regardless of what they did.

There are certain lines you don't cross when it comes to spirituality, and you should never mess with black magick or dark energy. I'm a firm believer that "like attracts like", and I'm sure to this day, the woman who sent this entity is living a reality that reflects her own negativity, jealousy and spitefulness.

Crystals for psychic protection and shielding

Now, we can't always know when we're going to encounter psychic vampires, negative people or malevolent spirits, but we can protect ourselves using crystals, sacred herbs and sound clearing tools. I do not believe crystals can hold evil energy within them, but I do believe their spiritual vibration can be used to amplify a person's intention, whether that is good or bad.

Crystals are created by Mother Nature using the 4 elements – wind, fire, water and earth – and hold within them only the highest of pure white-light energy and healing properties. A significant number of people carry the misconception that black crystals are evil, attract supernatural energy, are used by witches, satanic occult rituals or are the work of the devil. I find this concept humorous because any crystal colour or shape can be used for any intention or spiritual practice. In fact, black crystals are the most spiritually protective of them all, so embrace their grounding goodness without fear.

Crystals can be placed anywhere in your home for protection against negativity. However, I find the following ways to use them the most effective:

- ☾ Create a protection crystal grid around your property by burying a crystal in every corner of your outdoor boundaries.
- ☾ Place a crystal in the 4 corners of each room in your home.
- ☾ Use black crystals at any entry point or doorway to deter negativity from entering.
- ☾ Place a crystal on any window ledge to deflect negative energy out.
- ☾ Place a crystal in your bra or pocket or wear it in jewellery form to shield your aura wherever you travel.

 Walk in Beauty

Top tip: With any protection method you choose, it's essential to program the crystals with your intention and regularly cleanse them to release any toxic energy they may have absorbed for you.

The following are the top spiritually protective crystals.

Black tourmaline

Key phrase: Protection talisman.

Purpose: This beautiful black crystal has long been used by Native Americans to ward off evil, ill-wishing and spells. Black tourmaline is deeply grounding, eases anxiety, offers spiritual protection and provides our root chakra with stability.

Black onyx

Key phrase: Healing and empowerment.

Purpose: This ancient crystal healer has been used for centuries to deflect unwanted and stagnant energy, while helping us overcome unhealthy addictions. Black onyx deters negative energy away from our aura.

Black obsidian

Key phrase: Magick and peace.

Purpose: The glossy and reflective surface of this crystal makes her a much-loved stone in magick rituals and scrying. Black obsidian shields us from low-vibrating energy as we delve into the higher spiritual realms, and it dissipates feelings of irritability and restlessness by replacing them with positive, peaceful and white-light energy.

Smoky quartz

Key phrase: Paranormal protection.

Purpose: Wonderful for placing in the bedroom because the protective vibration eases nightmares and insomnia and deflects unwanted paranormal visits (because we all know that spiritual entities always appear at night). Invokes feelings of security as she protects us from psychic attacks and evil energy. Smoky quartz clusters have the ability to transform the energy within our spirit and home into positive and balanced energy.

 Walk in Beauty

Black jasper

Key phrase: Earth connection and nurturing.

Purpose: Jaspers come in many different colours, but I'm specifically highlighting black jasper for protection. All jaspers are deeply connected to Mother Earth and her grounding energy ions, which offer balance and stability. Black jasper will empower your thoughts, banish bad energy and will open your eyes to those who aren't genuine and those who are trustworthy.

Additional methods to shield yourself from negative energy include:

- ☾ distancing yourself from their drama and actions, or they will continue to drain you
- ☾ not feeling obliged to say "yes" to invites or feel you need to listen to their conversation
- ☾ being strong and not allowing anyone to encroach your personal space (aura surrounds)
- ☾ setting yourself clear boundaries and sticking to them regardless of whom it may offend
- ☾ not allowing their energy to lower your own vibration, even if they try intimidating or criticising you.

The bottom line is, you may need to end certain relationships if you feel someone's energy and underlying intentions are no longer aligning with you and your happiness. This may be difficult if they are family, a friend or coworker, but it's the best action.

Speaking of psychic vampires and their motives, I feel like I need to address the subject of "haters" out there. Like with anything we do in life, there will always be positive and negative people by our side. Our shining light, talent and enthusiasm will often attract criticism or dislike from others, even if we don't deserve it.

We don't expect everyone to like us, even if we try to be the kindest person on the planet. Most people will experience having "haters" at some point in their life. Now, there is nothing wrong with instantly disliking someone as this naturally happens and often for reasons we don't quite understand. I sometimes believe it stems from a previous lifetime and the interactions you had with that individual.

I never send ill-wishing or negative energy towards anyone as I'm a firm believer in karma. I choose to manifest goodness out into the universe rather than hate. Like attracts like so it's important to make love, not war!

 Walk in Beauty

Social media is a melting pot for keyboard warriors, haters, judgemental people, and good and bad reviews. Our social media pages are well-established, and we have a wonderful interaction with our people. I work hard and spend countless hours daily replying to emails, messages, comments and, yes, "hate".

This constant communication with everyone occurs every day (including weekends), and anyone with a small business will understand this. You never truly get away from your work, so it's essential you love what you do to avoid becoming burnt out.

The handful of hate we've received over the years has forced me to block people from our pages because I won't tolerate anyone running down our website, products, my family or disrespecting my work as a healer and businesswoman. I'm the type of person who must reply to love or hate messages, and when I encounter rude individuals, I will speak my truth, and often others don't like it.

I've encountered people who aren't even customers (they've never bought anything or received a service from us) yet spread hate and start arguments anyway. I question their motive and how they can dislike us in the first place if I've never had an interaction with them.

"Tall poppy syndrome" is alive and well, my friends, and you will encounter people who don't have the courage or motivation to push themselves to try to achieve their own goals in life. As a result, they see others who've succeeded and they express jealousy instead of kind words or encouragement. But what these people fail to see is what happens behind the scenes and the countless hours that are invested into making a dream a reality. Nothing worthwhile comes easy, and I believe this.

Usually, the people who are projecting hate and uneducated remarks rarely show their identity, have no profile photo, and have no business credentials themselves. I take criticism, and not everyone is going to be happy with a product, our service or our website design (believe it or not, I've had a couple of people say they hate the layout and colours).

One nasty person took their hatred one step further and created a Facebook post dedicated to highlighting the 'grammar typo' I made on our website. Oh no, I'm human and made a mistake, someone condemn me for my error! With thousands of items uploaded onto our website, it's bound to happen eventually. Is it seriously worth complaining and being negative about though? I find behaviour like this incredibly petty and immature.

 Walk in Beauty

I've had to distance myself from people, personally and professionally, because I've noticed some people want to be on your page simply to stalk you, even though they can't stand what you represent. When you recognise those people in your life who're projecting negative energy to you, you need to distance yourself from them (block them if necessary) because you need to protect your energy, aura and mental health.

You can only shine your light for so long before the draining energy of others takes its toll on you. As mentioned in the section on psychic vampires, this is your reminder to vibrate higher than the negative people around you and to not invest your valuable energy into entertaining their views and opinions. Instead, run as fast as you can away from them.

I have unsubscribed people from our newsletters when I intuitively feel they have underlying negative intentions and motives. I have also cancelled orders based on rude or abrupt emails I've received from customers. I'm not a money-driven person so losing a few sales over the years doesn't faze me in the slightest. I trust my instincts every time. I would rather connect with like-minded people who cherish our products, and I believe that is a smart business move.

I'm living my best life, I'm happily married, I have a beautiful family, gorgeous hounds, I'm surrounded by nature, and I'm so grateful for our little house in the Hinterland. I don't need anyone's negative drama, so I speak my mind and let their negative energy go. Out of sight and out of mind, that's what works best for me.

It's essential to take regular breaks from social media if you can because it can become overwhelming. Being an e-commerce business, I don't really have this option as it's a necessity to be present, available and to interact with people. I rarely post on my personal Facebook page but it's a requirement of having a business page. I enjoy connecting with a handful of loyal friends and family members but generally only on a weekly basis. I prefer living in the here and now and enjoying life around me.

For what it's worth, my advice (based on what I've learnt over the past 6 years of running a business social media page) is, "Don't compare yourself to others, and don't worry if your post only receives a few likes." Those interactions are your true people right there! I would take a handful of genuine and supportive people over a million fake likes and comments any day.

So many businesses buy fake likes on their pages, and it's often to feed their ego and make them appear larger and

 Walk in Beauty

more "successful" than they truly are. It's a common and sad occurrence to see. I encourage you to be happy with what you have and where you are right now in your life or business journey.

Just because someone seems more popular than you, has a more exciting life, travels the world, and takes hundreds of photos in fields of flowers, seeming like they have it all together ... remember, you're only seeing a snippet of their life.

I choose to march to the beat of my own drum, and I walk the walk without worrying about what others are doing because they don't affect me or my business. Choose to put yourself first because you are worth it. You are not being conceited and you are not being ego-driven; rather, you are being confident in yourself and authentic!

Good and Evil

All things in the world are two,
in our minds we are two – good and evil.
With our eyes we see two things –
things that are fair and things that are ugly...
We have the right hand that strikes
and makes for evil, and the left hand
full of kindness, near the heart.
One foot may lead us to an evil way,
the other foot may lead us to good.
So are all things two, all two.

Eagle Chief (Letakots-Lesa), late 19th century. Pawnee.

Chapter 11

Support from the higher realms and Great Spirit

I love talking about Great Spirit and spirituality in general to anyone who will listen. I have a chat with my ancestors, spirit guides and spirit animals every morning during my four-direction ritual, and I thank them for the blessings I have each night before I drift off to sleep.

Even if we think our spirit guides aren't listening, they always are! They watch us, support us and offer us guidance through signs and messages. Sometimes we may unintentionally miss the most obvious signs from our guides, and this can occur when we're busy, stressed and our mind is blocked.

As we all know, we can't choose our spirit guides; rather, they choose us based on what we need to learn in our lifetime. Below, I'm going to share my knowledge and experiences about the spirit world, in the hopes it will help you on your spiritual journey.

Spirit animals

Spirit animals always walk beside us during our lifetime here on Mother Earth. You may have one special spirit animal who remains with you for your entire life, but more often than not you will have a few different animals who appear at different stages of your journey to help you navigate obstacles, lessons, spiritual growth and life events.

Spirit animals support us in overcoming difficult times, periods of uncertainty, self-doubt, grief and loss, and they help us tune into our higher self. They often send us signs like recurring themes, images and songs, random words popping into our head, and even feelings in our body. We all have the ability to "sense" energy around us, and I often "feel" it.

Spirit animals don't always reveal themselves, and I have only ever known two of mine. The first experience with one of my spirit animals was several years ago. He was a little bear who appeared in our old house and in the kitchen of all places. Ashley and I were talking, and I abruptly jumped and fell into the cupboard in front of me because a little bear – the size of a small dog – stopped right before me at my feet!

I jumped out of the way without thinking, to avoid crashing into him. We both laughed when Ashley asked what I was

doing, and I said jumping out of Spirit Bear's way. I realise this sounds a little crazy, but it was as clear as day when he appeared to me. He then vanished as quickly as he appeared.

My other spirit animal appeared to me shortly before I began writing this book. He is a little wolf that has been guiding me along my chosen path for this stage in my journey. According to folklore and spiritual teachings, spirit animals are believed to make themselves known to us when they feel we are ready to wholeheartedly listen to their teachings and spiritual guidance.

Spirit guides

Spirit guides are beautiful soulful energies that reside in the higher spiritual realms. They always have our best intentions in mind and are our greatest supporters and protectors. Spirit guides may be human or non-human energy. Non-human means they have never been in a human form or walked upon the Earth; they are entirely spiritual beings.

I believe in both forms of spirit guides, and I also believe that we may have a past-life connection to the guides who were once human. For example, one of your spirit guides may have been your mother, father, child, spouse or best friend in a past life, and the connection between you both is still present. However, like with any spiritual concept, we all have our views and beliefs depending on our religious, spiritual and cultural backgrounds.

Regardless of what you believe, it's a wonderful practice to communicate daily with your guides, even if you don't know their identity, name or gender. It's important to not give up or become disheartened when working with spirit because the signs and messages from your guides are there, you just haven't tuned into them yet or you may need to work on developing your psychic gifts and intuition.

If you struggle to recognise the signs your guides are leaving you, try using a crystal and journal each night to support your intention to connect more deeply with the higher spiritual realms. Just like with anything in life, you need to be consistent and dedicated to your prayers, meditation or journalling because these practices will help your intuition decipher those cryptic and symbolic messages our guides pass onto us.

Meditation is essential to bring stillness into your mind and for opening your third eye chakra. When you can clear your mind of racing thoughts and distractions, you're already on your way to connecting with the divine energy of spirit in your mind and body. When you are grounded and peaceful,

 Walk in Beauty

the energy flowing from your root to crown chakra helps you ascend spiritually while remaining protected.

Clairvoyants and mediums

Chances are you've visited a psychic, medium or clairvoyant at some point during your life. If you're reading my book, own crystals and spiritual paraphernalia, and have an interest in the cosmic universe, it's only natural to gravitate towards people who embody and work with spirit on a daily basis.

Clairvoyants and psychic mediums are miraculous people who can connect with the higher realms, spirits and nature spirits. They receive images, words, insights, visions, energies or feelings from the spirit world that they then relay to us. The trick, however, is to find those who are legitimate and masters of their spiritual craft.

I'm fortunate to have found two women in the spiritual field whom I have the highest respect for. The messages and insights they have passed on to me over the years have helped get me to where I am today. Not all of my readings have been positive, let me tell you! But that's life and we all experience that ominous energy of the "The Tower" at some point.

Chapter 11

Here are a few insights that have flowed through from various readings over the years that still give me goosebumps each time I reflect on them or relay them to others.

My first reading was many moons ago, long before we lived in Eumundi, but we always visited the markets. The first reading was when I had just started our business and experienced a major setback, involving us setting up an entirely new website to replace the previous one that disappeared overnight. Safe to say, I was feeling discouraged by the stressful situation because our sales and online presence had disappeared due to the glitch.

Fast forward a couple of days, and thankfully we had booked a long weekend away. I visited Eumundi markets and went to a psychic medium named Karine, and without knowing anything about me besides my first name, the reading she gave me was spot on. Every card she turned over was beyond accurate, and I was scared but also intrigued! Karine advised me that the website glitch had to happen because we had to structure our business a different way to make it a success (I wish my guides could have told me this in the first place, ha-ha).

I was frustrated but her words provided me with hope, and I used that energy to upload thousands of photos and

 Walk in Beauty

product listings once again. It took many months and long days and nights to build up our new website. I cried, I had meltdowns, I swore and I threw tantrums along the way.

I still do swear daily as I find it releases my throat chakra and helps me remain balanced, and no I'm not kidding! Releasing anger, frustration, stress and irritability is perfectly normal because we can't be "Positive Pollyannas" every day of the week (this pun is for my friend Amber because this is what she calls me, ha-ha).

I wanted to give up, but my family wouldn't let me and nor did my spirit guides, so I trusted them and kept progressing. A few years later, I had my next significant reading with Karine, which related to moving houses. At the time, our business was stable and flowing along with me and Wayne at the helm.

We decided we wanted to move to the Hinterland and downsize our large house to a smaller house with more land. That way we could expand the business and give our stock its own warehouse space instead of using the space in our home. I like to keep the two separate now we are a larger business, and I want to relax without seeing work in front of me in our cosy little house. We had been searching for months to no avail. Nothing suited us, and I began doubting that it would ever happen.

Chapter 11

But my reading with Karine revealed we were going to move very soon, and she told me my spirit guides were making it happen, even though I was receiving no signs from them. She also advised me the house would be a no. 8, revealed part of the street name, and said it would have great energy, and the previous owner would be a woman who lived alone. This was pretty intense and specific information.

A few weeks later we were visiting the Hinterland and looking at an open home (which again wasn't for us), but, as we were leaving, we drove past a street and out of the corner of my eye up the hill, I noticed a pole house. It looked so unique and immediately stood out to me, and it also had a real estate sign out front. I told Wayne to make a detour so we could get a better look, but he wanted to get home, so we didn't turn around.

When we got home, I couldn't get the glimpse of the house out of my mind, but we didn't know the street name or anything to help us narrow down the search. I immediately jumped on the laptop and began researching houses for sale in Eumundi, while hoping I could find it based on memory. I did – it was no.8, and it was for sale!

This was our house, I just knew it. I called the real estate agent that night and she met us the following day, which

 Walk in Beauty

was a Sunday morning. We left early and there was a torrential thunderstorm with such severity we had to pull over on the side of the freeway (it was a frightening experience). I had my rune in my bra at the time (I drew it in the early morning), and it was Raidho, which is symbolic of moving forward to a chosen destination, evolution and strength. It had to be right!

I said to Wayne that perhaps we shouldn't keep driving in the weather conditions, but of course we did. When we pulled up to the front of the house, I immediately told Wayne we were buying it. He advised me to not speak this truth too early to the realtor.

The moment we walked in, I knew it was the house Karine had told me about. We transferred a deposit within hours, did the necessary inspections, and sold our beautiful family home of 20 years within 9 days of placing it on the market.

I always vowed I would never leave that home until the day I died, but it just goes to show that things do change – this is a necessary part of shaping our current life journey. It takes us to where we need to be. We can't remain the same or we would cease to learn new lessons and experiences we need to evolve. Everything moved so fast and went through without incident because this was where we were supposed to be for this next chapter of our life.

The moral of the story is to never give up on a dream because even though it may take years (like ours did), it will be so worth it in the end. Your spirit guides know what you need, so put your faith in their hands and allow them to guide you.

My recent reading in 2023 with Karine revealed my book, which I had just started writing (and which she had no idea about), as well as feathers, nature and staying on my spiritual path for the next several months, no detours permitted. Karine advised I would remain blessed and protected. Once again, all the cards were accurate and, as predicted, here you are reading the book I felt guided to write.

The next stop was Lesley Ann, a clairvoyant who creates spirit guide artwork, whom I met at the Brisbane Mind, Body, Spirit festival. I had no idea who she was, but I knew I needed to see her. She proceeded to draw my spirit guide, who is a beautiful Native American man named "Gray Wolf", who also has a little wolf by his side who is my spirit animal.

The colours of my aura and the energy surrounding his image are blue and purple tones. These colours make sense because blue and purple are healing colours and are associated with those who practise Reiki. I'm not surprised

having Gray Wolf as one of my guides because of my Native American ancestry. But to actually see a beautiful artwork of him and to hang it in the Reiki corner of my bedroom is such a special feeling.

I feel so much gratitude to him and my little wolf guide for revealing themselves to me. The little wolf is described as being gentle in energy and not an alpha by any means. He leads me along the path I currently need to be on like a personal guide dog. It makes sense that I would have a wolf because I have always howled at the moon and am obsessed with watching them on social media reels.

Something else that gave me goosebumps during my reading was when Lesley Ann asked me whether I had ever felt tickles or breezes around my neck. Indeed, I had! One night I was working at the table and nearly jumped off my chair when I felt that someone was touching me on the neck. My body went into high alert and goosebumps broke out over my skin within a few moments.

I spun around quickly as I thought it was one of my family members trying to startle me as a joke because I was in deep concentration. But, no, Taylar was relaxing on the sofa on the other side of the living room. Lesley Ann went on to say this was Gray Wolf, who uses his feather to gain my attention and prompt me to move forward.

I was amazed at this revelation because I've experienced that feeling many times now, and this knowledge validated it for me. She went on to reveal little things that nearly made me fall off my chair (lol) and she was accurate in describing my daily four directions ritual to nature, my guides and ancestors.

Lesley told me that Gray Wolf asked me to dedicate a feather and special crystal to include in my ritual. No one apart from my immediate family know about my ritual besides all of you now, yet she was able to describe this without hesitation.

Lesley Ann also told me Gray Wolf wanted me to wear a feather around my neck as feathers are sacred symbols in Native American culture, which symbolise freedom, strength, power, and which help us connect to the spirit world and Creator. This is my spiritual belief.

As soon as I arrived home, I bought a frame for the artwork and started thinking of what style feather to silversmith, and, of course, I made myself a selenite wand using the natural bird feathers I collect. When my spirit guides speak, I always listen! I feel that my guides are smiling at my efforts following their contact because I've been feeling incredibly uplifted since connecting with their presence and knowing what they look like.

 Walk in Beauty

Always try to make time to talk to your spirit guides and spirit animals, and of course all of those who have transitioned into the spirit world.

Do you ever feel or recognise little signs from your spirit guides or spirit animal? They make you feel incredibly secure and at peace once you know it's them, don't they?

If you've ever wondered what your spirit guides/animals look like, take my advice and seek out an experienced person in this field and place your trust in the connection they hold with the spirit world. Your guide may be wanting you to reach out and take an interest in their presence and signs. Perhaps this paragraph is your prompt from the universe to delve deeper and put a face and name to your spirit guides and animals.

Our loved ones are alive and well in the higher realms, and they are watching and cheering us on from the sidelines. I share the same belief as Native Americans that there is no death; it's just a changing of worlds. We don't say goodbye, we say, "Until next time because we will meet again."

As Karine always reminds me, there is no time in the spirit world, for it is irrelevant to them. Imagine how freeing that would be? Never running to a schedule and never checking the time ... just amazing!

Chapter 11

Divine synchronicity

This is that feeling when everything is falling into place as it should be. We have ideas, see signs and know we are going in the right direction. These seemingly innocent coincidences are a sign that has been sent from your spirit guides, the universe or loved ones. They assure us that we are getting our life right. It's like the ultimate pat on the back from the spirit world, and I love it.

Those signs also come from the living; friends, family, even strangers you cross paths with. They are there at that time for a reason, a lesson, to make us take notice. Never disregard these little signs or occurrences – they are trying to gain your attention.

This next prompt for me happened one morning when I was brushing my teeth, like any other day before work. Taylar was the one who got this ball rolling for me. She walked in and asked me out of the blue what else would I do as a job if I didn't have our business of crystals and healings. Without hesitating and speaking with toothpaste in my mouth, I said, "Silversmithing!" Then she looked up lessons and within a few hours I was booked in to start learning. What just happened?

 Walk in Beauty

I took Ashley along as I wanted moral support. I consider myself a slow learner and felt awkward being partly deaf (I didn't have my hearing aids at that point, so I misheard a lot of words), so she could help me if I missed something in translation during a lesson (nothing is worse than replying something that has nothing to do with the conversation, lol). However, I absolutely loved the experience and made a ring with a lot of help from a wonderful man named Nick. He has been silversmithing for over 40 years.

He picked up on my love of, yep you guessed it, Native American-style jewellery, and we created my pieces from there. Of course, I used turquoise. Next, Wayne decided to come to a lesson, and he enjoyed it as much as me. So, we both worked our weekly lessons into our work schedule. Nick became my new mentor, and he was amazing. He encouraged us, he explained things simply and was proud of our achievements. Having one-on-one lessons was simply ideal for me.

Next, we proceeded to buy all the fun things like equipment and tools and, of course, sterling silver and crystal cabochons. Wayne was so determined he even built us a little cedarwood studio on our property. I named her "SweetGrass Studio", which is symbolic of peace, blessings, love and good energy. You don't want to silversmith in your home, trust me! It's dirty, messy and those smells of patina, sulphur and flux are eye watering at the best of times.

We made mistakes, we got frustrated, we melted things down time after time for a few months. Then it happened – it started coming together the more hours we spent practising. We were now confident to offer our jewellery designs on our website as the support we received when I'd share progress photos on our social media platforms was just beautiful.

We truly have the most wonderful people who follow and purchase from us. Many have become friends that I chat with weekly. So, like my ancestors before me, this was another skill I learnt. The feeling of making jewellery that others love, and wear, is indescribable; they carry a little piece of creativity, determination and love that we pour into every unique piece.

The moral of this story is to always be open to thinking outside the box you are in. Be in a circle instead. In a circle everything is even – there is no beginning or end, it continues to flow. All these seemingly random conversations, dreams or fleeting thoughts are signs from the universe and your spirit guides. They are gaining your attention by using another "human" to make you take note of what you can actually accomplish if you are prompted.

Walk in Beauty

The only thing you have to lose is your time and energy. Don't put yourself in the position years down the track thinking, *I wish I tried silversmithing, art, sewing, music, writing*... You may succeed or you may find it wasn't exactly what you hoped for, but you never know unless you give it a go. We all have a talent for something and all you need to do is find what yours is. I believe these interests and hobbies all stem from previous life experiences and we have never quite forgotten them.

From the beginning there were drums,
beating out world rhythm –
the booming, never failing tide on the beach;
the four seasons, gliding smoothly one from the other;
when the birds come, when they go,
the bear hibernating for his winter sleep.
Unfathomable the why, yet all in perfect time.
Watch the heartbeat in your wrist –
A precise pulsing beat of life's drum –
with loss of timing you are ill.

Jimalee Burton, also known as Ho-Chee-Nee, 1974. Cherokee.

Chapter 12

Making magick with candles

Candles are wonderful, magickal tools that are used for various spiritual purposes and in mindful-based practices. I always burn a crystal during a Reiki healing as it allows me to keep my sage bundle smouldering for purification of my space.

Candles carry the element of fire within them, which is symbolic of rebirth, destruction, renewal, purification and warmth. I see candles as a reflection of our inner light burning bright. Remember to never let anyone dim your light!

Candles help create a harmonious mood and ambience in our space and encourage us to relax when combined with crystals and essential oils. The combination of herbs, crystals and spirituality naturally invokes inner healing, relaxation and calming emotions within us. You may choose candles with crystal inclusions that compliment the essential oil blended into their soy wax. These are a perfect healing duo for your home or entire family to benefit from.

Another type of candle is the "wish" or "intention" candles, and these usually have a quick burn time of around 1 to 2 hours, so they may be burnt for specific purposes like magick spells, prayers, manifesting or sending your wishes out into the universe.

Some people believe you need to let the candle burn in its entirety, but I don't necessarily follow this rule. I believe that by lighting a candle, connecting with the flame and allowing your thoughts to be heard by the universe, the metaphysical action is immediate. Of course, your prayer or wish may not transpire into your life that quickly!

The old tradition of blowing out your birthday candles and making a wish rings true in many cultures. Candles have a powerful intent when used correctly and can offer you colour healing (see Chapter 4 for more details on colour benefits). I'm going to highlight some of the most popular candle colours that can be used in your spell work or intention setting. I also love writing a little mantra to use with each colour candle.

In my experience, it's best to keep your thoughts and prayers simple. Complex words and chapters aren't

 Walk in Beauty

required for your prayers to be heard. Using a mantra helps to empower your thoughts outwards into the universe and encourage you to keep believing in yourself and miracles.

Below are some of my favourite mantras, but feel free to improvise and write your own too as it's an enjoyable practice. I end my mantra or prayer with the Cherokee phrase "A'ho", which means, "I understand" or "amen" when used in prayers. You should use whatever spiritual or cultural phrase you believe in or identify with.

Black candles

Key purpose: Protection against negative energy and evil.

Black candles bring grounding and a feeling of inner security. Burn them for clearing yourself of stagnant energy or feelings of anxiety. Black candles will purify your home and allow you to ground more deeply with Mother Earth and all her healing properties.

Crystal combinations: The energy of black candles is amplified when using black obsidian, which offers grounding and protection, and black tourmaline to ward off malevolent entities and negative energy.

Mantra:

*Candle dark, candle bright,
Banish any shadows, ill-wishing, and evil,
By the element of fire, I walk my path in healing light.
A'ho.*

Blue candles

Key purpose: Healing, calming and clear communication.

Blue candles help to encourage feelings of forgiveness, loyalty, and to speak truthfully always. Burn blue candles if you're seeking clarification, need to clear your thoughts, to enhance a deeper understanding of situations, or to receive any answers you may be seeking. The colour blue helps activate your throat chakra and encourages you to use your voice with intention.

Crystal combinations: The energy of blue candles is enhanced when using crystals like angelite, for increasing connection with the angelic and higher spiritual realms, and celestite, for invoking feelings of peace and clarity within the mind and spirit.

 Walk in Beauty

Mantra:

I honour my ancestors before me,
Share your wisdom and intuition,
I open my mind and emotions to the higher realms.
A'ho.

Red candles

Key purpose: Passion, strength and courage.

Red candles bring passion into our life and help empower our actions and creative thoughts. Burn them for attracting power, love and romance as they awaken our root chakra.

Crystal combinations: Red candles work wonderfully with carnelian, for increasing passion and vitality, and red jasper, for amplifying life-force energy and fertility.

Mantra:

I call the goddess of love,
Share with me courage and strength,
Burn bright and surround me with love and passion.
A'ho.

White candles

Key purpose: Purity, rebirth and hope.

White candles bring feelings of renewal and self-growth. Burn them if you're seeking hope, miracles or faith. The colour white helps open your body and mind to receiving the illuminating universal white-light energy for all-over body healing.

Crystal combinations: White candles work beautifully with selenite by invoking lunar and feminine energy and enhancing your connection with your intuition. Lemurian seed crystals also amplify the intention of white crystals by opening your mind to access inner truths, wisdom and personal growth.

Mantra:

*I call in universal white light,
Surround and illuminate my aura,
Shine bright in moon and starlight.
A'ho.*

 Walk in Beauty

Pink candles

Key purpose: Love, compassion and understanding.

Pink candles bring compassion and gentle energy into our mind and spirit. Burn them for surrounding yourself with nurturing and loving energy, to increase self-love and to attract love from another, and to receive healing within your heart.

Crystal combinations: Pink crystals paired with rose quartz offer unconditional love, and paired with rhodonite they offer balance within your yin–yang energy, and emotional healing.

Mantra:

I call upon Mother Earth,
Connect me with love, nurture and peace,
May I find bliss and share compassion with all.
A'ho.

Yellow and orange candles

Key purpose: Positivity, abundance and happiness.

Yellow and orange candles naturally bring vitality, boost our spirit and help us remain upbeat. Burn them for attracting health, goodwill and abundance. The bright colours connect with our solar plexus for stamina and optimism.

Crystal combinations: Yellow and orange crystals resonate with citrine, to increase feelings of bliss, joy and high vibrations, and orange calcite, for connecting with our sexuality, creativity and happiness.

Mantra:

I call upon the four directions,
Bring me creativity and abundance,
Burn bright like our life creator, Father Sun.
A'ho.

 Walk in Beauty

Tis mine to be in love with life,
And mine to hear the robins sing;
Tis mine to live apart from strife,
And kneel to flowers blossoming.

Alex Posey, 19th century Creek poet. Creek.

Chapter 13

Practising divination

Divination is a spiritual practice anyone can do. Despite what others say, you don't need to be a psychic medium or witch (even though we're often labelled as witches) to delve into the art of divination. Women are powerful, intuitive beings who have overcome centuries of despair, judgement and ridicule for having intuitive magickal powers and otherworldly knowledge.

Intuition is a large part of your spiritual path, and it's this inner knowing that we often cannot explain how or when it occurs. It flows naturally to us during certain stages of our life, and we shouldn't second guess it. When you practise listening to your intuition, you open your world up to a place of divine synchronicities.

However, there are some things to be mindful of when engaging in spiritual and divination work, particularly good and bad energy. I believe lower-vibrational beings lurk in

 Walk in Beauty

the shadows waiting for a porthole to be opened during spiritual practices.

I love nothing more than using my white sage smudge bundle to cleanse my surrounds and divination tools before and after use as the smoke is empowering, clearing and protective. Always use spiritual protection when performing any divination practice, and it's advisable to hold off if you're feeling lethargic, emotionally and mentally depleted, and not your usual self.

So, let's explore the most popular divination practices and provide insight into how they can be used.

Pendulums

Pendulums help us tune in to what has not yet happened and, in most cases, the future events that are awaiting us to discover and live. Think of those feelings of déjà vu that have happened; you feel like you've already done this scenario before ... Pendulums are energy amplifiers that work with our intuitive energy and higher self. I find pendulums one of the easiest forms of divination to learn and use whether you are a complete beginner or well-experienced in divination work.

To cleanse and charge your pendulum before and after use, lower it into the rising smoke from your sage bundle and then circle the smoke around your head and hands.

Be careful when smudging yourself as I've burnt many clothes from the hot ash falling on me, and I have no idea until the heat warms through to my skin!

Once you've smudged your pendulum and self, prepare your pendulum for the highest of good intentions and protection before you commence with any spiritual work, healing or meditation. When you finish your session, cleanse the energies that your pendulum has absorbed from you and your surrounds.

Pendulums are useful for dowsing and scrying, in tarot readings, and for investigating paranormal activity. I've never used one to investigate a haunting, but I'm told by others that the pendulum swings wildly in a spirit's presence.

Alternatively, you can use your pendulum for "yes and no" charts to determine answers and gain clarity about situations, or for establishing a connection with the higher spiritual realms. Whatever you use your pendulum for, ensure you close your session by thanking both the universe and your spirit guides for their protection.

 Walk in Beauty

Scrying mirrors

Scrying mirrors are a mystical gazing tool full of magick! Scrying means to look or see a glimpse of an image reflected back to you using a reflective surface. You may have a question about something, such as your career, purchasing a home, a relationship, or your ongoing health, and scrying is a way of glimpsing into your future.

In most scrying practices a candle is lit prior to beginning as it serves as a link to the spirit world while you gaze into the flame. Other ways of scrying include the use of water, a mirror or crystal balls.

Scrying with water can be done by filling a bowl of water or sitting in front of a still pond or lake and gazing at the reflective surface until you see an image flash before you. Water scrying is perfect for anyone who feels a strong resonance to the cleansing, calming and recharging energy associated with the element of water.

Scrying with a crystal ball or using mirrors in your home are also effective ways to delve into a meditative state of mind and connect with the spirit world. As with all divination, you will find your mind naturally drifting into a trance-like state when you quieten your thoughts and connect with your higher self.

Runes

I love runes! I discovered runes many years ago and resonated with them after my first use. I am self-taught and found runes easy to work with due to the natural connection I feel towards their energy and symbology.

Rune stones are used to predict the future and explore where you are in the present moment. The stones come in a set of 24 ancient alphabetic symbols and are made from different materials, such as crystals, wood, stones or glass.

Runes are generally stored in a pouch or trinket box; I choose to keep mine in a copper offering bowl, which keeps them charged between uses. Copper has its own unique vibration, which opens energy pathways in your body and in your surrounds. Therefore, it effectively charges crystals and our personal energy if we hold or wear it.

You will need to connect with your runes prior to initial use as your energy needs to be compatible and vibrating on the same wavelength for the runes to be accurate. Dedicate time to clearing your runes, charging them in the sunlight, and blessing them with the highest of good energy and intention. I recommend not allowing anyone besides yourself to touch or use your runes as they are attuned to your energy.

 Walk in Beauty

Legend says that when you cast your runes you should do so facing the sun. Again, like any spiritual practice, choose what works well for you. When using your runes, you may choose to cast them on a soft cloth, velvet material, altar table, divination board, in the dirt or the grass, etc. I use a Wicca wooden board or my bed to cast my runes on because both surfaces hold my energy within them.

You may use whatever surface feels right for you, but keep in mind that the same surface should be used each time, if possible, as this helps the energy remain strong and provides a familiar sacred space for you to connect with.

With the numerous rune layouts to try, I recommend investing in a good book about them as it will be invaluable. I always keep my book close to my runes so I can refer to it as needed. I love a quick intuitive pick from my bowl of runes in the morning to gain insight into the energy for the day ahead. I then either place that rune on display or pop it into my bra to remind myself of the energy surrounding me.

Or, if I have a question that I awake with or am struggling to find clarity about, I draw a rune as a message of guidance. Runes are seriously accurate little divination tools so be prepared because they may even call you out on certain things you need to change or stop doing!

Candle gazing

As we know, flames hold the element of fire, the symbology of rebirth, and rising from the ashes to embark on a new beginning. Candles help relax our mind for meditation, healings and divination practices. They provide a focus point, which allows our mind to focus on a single object rather than wandering off with a million different thoughts and scenarios.

Your mind, body and spirit need to be in a relaxed and meditative state before you begin gazing into the candle's flame. I often experience a wave of deep relaxation when candle gazing, to the point where I could actually fall asleep (I haven't yet fallen asleep but feel completely at ease within my mind and body).

As you gaze into the flame with an open mind, allow your candle to show you glimpses of images dancing in the flame. You may feel a shift in the energy around you, your spirit animal may appear in the flame, or you may enter a black void of nothing besides deep relaxation, and that in itself can be incredibly rewarding.

If you wish to use candles for specific purposes and intention, you can choose them based on their colour. You may like to refer to my colour therapy section in Chapter 4.

 Walk in Beauty

Oracle and tarot decks

Oracle and tarot decks are always popular, and for good reason too! The decks are collections of beautiful artworks, symbology and insights for us to use as often as we need.

Oracle and tarot decks will often surprise us with their revelations and can be uncannily accurate too. But make no mistake, the two decks are different with their spiritual insights and advice.

Oracle decks are far gentler in their divination approach and tend to feature cards that help inspire, motivate and nurture us on our spiritual path and current circumstances. They focus on various subjects including self-love, body compassion, spirituality and ancestral healing.

Oracle cards will lift our spirit and mindset with a simple affirmation or mantra that we relate to. With oracle cards, you only need to choose 1–3 cards to receive answers or the wisdom you're seeking. This makes them easy to use and less complex than learning tarot because you don't need to memorise 78 card archetypes and meanings. Most oracle decks will include a little booklet with information about the cards and how to use them.

I also like to put my own spin on the card I've drawn to personalise it for me by allowing my intuition to step in. Do you do this too? After all, we are all at a different mindset and vibration from each other, so the same card is going to hold different interpretations for us all … It just makes sense to trust our intuition and instinct regarding the way the card symbology makes us feel and how it resonates with our current life situation.

Tarot decks, on the other hand, focus on the nitty-gritty aspects of our life and self and are a real wake-up call when we're seeking guidance or need a reality check. Tarot decks are more structured in their imagery with major and minor arcana symbology and universal archetypes, making them more complicated than oracle cards.

I tried multiple times to grasp tarot but just couldn't resonate with them. I do love receiving a tarot reading and, of course, for this I turn to our daughter Tarot Taylar as she is an expert in them! I always recommend buying a good in-depth tarot book because the knowledge within the pages will prove invaluable; there is a lot to learn. Invest your time into learning tarot before jumping straight into using a deck because in the long run it will be of greater benefit to you.

Before using an oracle or tarot pack, it's essential to bless them and connect yourself to their energy. They may be charged using a little crystal generator (clear quartz is my

first choice always) or in the sunshine before and after use. Leaving a crystal on or in the trinket box or pouch where you keep your cards when not in use is something Taylar and I both practise, ensuring our card decks are charged with positive and protective energy always.

Do you have a favourite you want to try after reading these divination practices? Perhaps you may have already mastered one of these and are keen to try the next! As you get more experienced, you may like to offer a reading or insight to your loved ones. It can be comforting for them, if they aren't familiar with these forms of divination, but most people love receiving signs from the universe and the heavens above. You will feel happy and content within yourself for sharing your talent with them too.

A'ho

Well, this brings us to the end of *Walk in Beauty with MoonstoneGypsyAU*.

I hope you have enjoyed learning about the various spiritual topics explored in this book and developed further insight into your own spiritual and metaphysical journey.

The insights shared from my professional and personal life are to remind and encourage you that nothing in this world can hold you back from pursuing a dream, regardless of the obstacles that surface along the way.

Never stop learning and opening yourself up to new knowledge and pathways in life because it keeps you on your toes, expands your awareness and helps you move forward in life, rather than remaining in a stagnant state.

Walk in beauty, Kelli. xx

Walk in Beauty

Walk proud. Walk straight. Let your thoughts race.

Walk proud, walk straight,
let your thoughts race with the blue wind,
but do not bare your soul to your enemies.

Patty Harjo.

About the author

Kelli has a love of all things spiritual and nature. Embarking on her crystal and Reiki journey many moons ago opened her eyes to a world of healing, magick and higher spiritual realms. This allowed her to create her own business, inspire others and heal hundreds of clients over the years.

Kelli resides with her family in the quirky Hinterland town of Eumundi, Australia. It's no secret Kelli spends her days drinking multiple coffees, eating chocolate and indulging in cake. She enjoys listening to loud '90s music, wearing cowboy boots and turquoise, and silversmithing in the studio with her husband. She enjoys gardening and cherishes her beloved hounds.

Social media platforms:

Facebook & Instagram: Moonstone Mystic Au

Website:

www.moonstonegypsyau.com

www.ingramcontent.com/pod-product-compliance
Lightning Source LLC
Chambersburg PA
CBHW040241010526
44107CB00065B/2822